APL

PRINCIPLES
IN FLEXIBLE
ASSESSMENT:
A PRACTICAL GUIDE

SECOND EDITION

Susan Simosko and Cathy Cook

**KOGAN
PAGE**

First published in 1991 as APL: *A Practical Guide for Professionals*
Reprinted in 1992 and 1993
This second edition published in 1996

Kogan Page Limited
120 Pentonville Road
London N1 9JN

British Library Cataloguing in Publication Data
A CIP record for this book is available from the British Library.

ISBN 0 7494 2099 5

Typeset by DP Photosetting, Aylesbury, Bucks
Printed and bound in Great Britain by
Biddles Ltd, Guildford and King's Lynn

Contents

CONTENTS

Preface to the Second Edition

Many changes have occurred since this book was first published in 1991:

- S/NVQs have become more widely accepted and integrated into the education and training infrastructure. More than a million S/NVQs have been awarded.
- Employers have invested in the implementation of standards and S/NVQs as a matter of good business practice. They have trained assessors, designated mentors and encouraged employees to take greater responsibility for their own learning and development in the workplace.
- Assessment practices have been reviewed, analysed and modified in many different contexts in order to reduce costs while still maintaining technical quality.
- Education and training providers have worked more collaboratively and Training and Enterprise Councils (TECs) have played a major role in cultivating regional access to flexible learning and assessment opportunities for large numbers of people.
- There has been a growing recognition that assessment is an intrinsic component of learning, not a stand-alone activity. Self-assessment has been emphasised as a critical component of the learning and assessment process.

In the centre of all this change there has been a fundamental shift in the concept and application of the accreditation of prior learning (APL). While once viewed by education and training organisations as a separate, stand-alone service, APL is now widely accepted as an essential, integrated component of all competence-based assessment systems. Hence our new title: *Applying APL Principles in Flexible Assessment: A Practical Guide.*

Diverse evidence, once viewed as relevant only to APL, is now considered a natural aspect of most competence-based assessment systems. As part of these systems, learners are expected to generate evidence in their ongoing effort to learn, develop and undergo assessment. The continuum of learning includes assessment and the continuum of assessment includes learning.

APL as a distinct process or a unique set of tools has all but disappeared in the UK, and in other parts of the world it is rapidly merging with more integrated assessment systems. In its place we find people referring to 'flexible assessment' methods, 'outcome-based assessment' or 'competence-based assessment'. The emphasis now is on the nature of the evidence and the role of the individual in generating that evidence, not a particular assessment process set apart from any others.

The shift in language reflects a belief that people can and do learn in everything they do; that at different points in time throughout their lives, they will come forward for assessment because they need or want a new credential, a new job, or to prepare themselves for future change. The tools by which they are assessed will vary depending on the context in which they are working and learning and they themselves will be able to determine, in many cases, the type of evidence they need to generate in order to demonstrate what they know and can do. No longer is assessment viewed as something that is *done* to an individual. Rather, in competence-based systems, the individual is increasingly viewed as a key partner in the assessment process.

As the diagram below illustrates, the individual is guided in the learning and assessment process by occupational standards or learning outcomes. As part of that process, many different strategies can be used to generate or contribute to evidence requirements: demonstration in the workplace or classroom; demonstration through simulations, special projects or assignments in work or training; or oral and written questioning. However, in the centre is the learner who, in many instances, begins the process by preparing a personal statement, developing a portfolio of diverse evidence, or requesting some other type of assessment that is in keeping with the context in which he or she is working and learning.

CONTINUUM OF ASSESSMENT

Learning outcomes   Occupational standards

Assessment by portfolio

Assessment on demand

Course assessment   Workplace assessment

| Demonstration | simulation or role play | project or assignment | examination – oral – written |

About the Second Edition

This second edition, then, has tried to capture the essence of these changes while at the same time retaining much of the material readers continue to find valuable. The new material in the book reflects:

- the widespread use of S/NVQs;
- the greater involvement of employers in the assessment process;
- the importance of self-assessment as part of a more learner-driven system;
- significant changes in language; and
- the integration of the concept of APL into the competence-based assessment system itself.

We have included a separate chapter on S/NVQs and some case studies. We have given greater emphasis to employers, training managers and human resource specialists as assessment professionals; we have changed the language to reflect the broadest possible concept of the application of APL principles, eg flexible assessment, competence-based assessment systems, learner-driven assessment processes. Finally, we have tried to keep our attention focused on the needs of the learners, whether they are working and learning in factories, offices, classrooms or elsewhere; whether they are generating external evidence from their waged or unwaged work, in their communities or homes; whether they are working independently, in groups or with a mentor or adviser; and whether they are working with or without the aid of technology.

As this second edition illustrates, the world of competence-based assessment continues to evolve. The concept of APL is centre stage now, enabling people from all walks of life both to value and receive recognition for their continuing learning achievements.

Susan Simosko and Cathy Cook
July 1996

Acknowledgments to the Second Edition

Thanks are extended to all those people who contributed to the first and second editions of this book, in particular Jonathan Stewart, Gloria Savage, our employer, TEC and education and training colleagues, and the hundreds of candidates around the world who have helped us to learn, develop and continue to see things in new ways.

Special thanks, too, are extended to Graham Debling and Tim Foster for their continued support, ideas and encouragement throughout the preparation of this second edition.

Susan Simosko and Cathy Cook
July 1996

Chapter 1

Assessment and APL: What's it all about?

Introduction

All over the world the drive is on to make better use of existing resources. Nowhere is this more true than in the area of human resource development. Educators, trainers, employers and government policy makers, regardless of nation, seem to be saying much the same thing: that as nations we must put individuals first and 'provide opportunities whereby everyone can make maximum use of their potential' (CBI, 1989).

Educators, trainers and other human resource development specialists are concerned that too much valuable time and effort is lost teaching people what they already know and can do. Growing numbers of employers regularly express concern that education and training take too much time and money and that their employees are away from work too frequently. At the same time, they readily admit their concern that individual employees are often demotivated, unwilling or ill-prepared to respond to future demands and changes within an industry. Government policy makers, too, grapple with the need to foster positive change in organisations, industry and individuals to ensure a viable economic future and a stable, equitable society for all.

Clearly in each context there are a number of ways these problems are being addressed, nationally, regionally and locally. The concept of recognising and accrediting what people already know and can do is having a profound impact on many of the

1

education and training solutions being developed today. This concept is called the Accreditation of Prior Learning (APL). In Britain, Australia, North America and elsewhere, professionals have introduced APL in an effort to motivate individuals, make more effective use of training resources, increase the flexibility of organisations, and cultivate attitudes that value life-long learning. In so doing, those who have introduced and delivered APL services have also enhanced their own professional development through acquiring new skills and working in changing environments with increasingly diverse groups of people.

APL: what is it?

The terminology

First, a word about the terms used to describe the process: in the USA, where much of the early work originated, the process is usually called 'prior learning assessment (PLA)'; in Australia, where the concept is just taking hold, the term most often used is the 'recognition of prior learning (RPL)'; and in the UK the words include not only 'accreditation of prior learning (APL)' but also 'accreditation of prior achievement (APA)' and 'assessment of prior experiential learning (APEL)'. A lot of energy has gone into getting the words right within each nation and context, but the basic concept remains the same: that through a systematic and valid assessment process, an individual's skills and knowledge can be formally recognised and credited, regardless of how, when or why they were obtained.

It is important to add that in many contexts the concept, procedures and tools of APL have become an integral part of flexible assessment or competence-based assessment systems. **There is no difference between the tools and procedures of competence-based assessment and those of APL.**

People have come to realise in fact that there is no other type of learning besides 'prior'. The concept of APL is simply another way of recognising that people learn throughout their lives and

2

in many different contexts. The assessment and accreditation process – by any name – only serves to recognise, honour and accredit that learning.

One thing APL surely is not: credit for life experience. People do not receive recognition or credit for what they experience in life. Although all that a person learns in life may be of value to that individual, in the assessment process it is the attainments, skills and knowledge, or competences* – all of which may have been attained experientially – that are recognised and credited. Although the basic concept seems clear enough, inappropriate terminology has led to many misunderstandings and a belief in some people that the process is a 'soft option' towards obtaining qualifications. Those who have been through the process or those professionals who have committed themselves to setting up a sound programme will know otherwise!

The original introduction of the words 'prior learning' was intended to emphasise that what was being assessed was outside – independent of – any particular *current* formal academic course. The increasingly blurred lines between 'training' and 'education' have put a strain on the word, for indeed, many people identify current learning from their work, employer-based training programmes or non-credit adult education courses.

The words themselves are not critical to the process, although indeed great efforts are being made around the world, in many different languages, to modify the term to more accurately reflect the process. Words such as 'flexible assessment' or 'learner-centred assessment' are emerging to suggest some of the more comprehensive changes in education and training around the world. Indeed, in many contexts, especially in the UK, the phrase APL is disappearing, not because the concept is irrelevant but because the emerging competence-based assessment system naturally absorbs the concept.

* Competences is a term which has been developed in Britain to refer to skills, knowledge and abilities. Other countries may use the word 'competencies'.

The concept

As a concept, the accreditation of prior learning acknowledges that much of what people know and can do can be recognised in some formal way towards accredited qualifications. It is built on the premise that people can and do learn throughout their lives – formally and informally, systematically and unsystematically – and that this uncertificated learning can be equated and measured against the same standards used to evaluate learners completing more traditional and formal learning programmes.

The type of recognition people receive varies with the context: sometimes it is in the form of credit towards a particular vocational or academic qualification; sometimes it is in the form of exemption from some portion of an educational or training programme; and almost always it is used as a development tool by both the individual undergoing the process and the educational or training providers offering the service.

Intrinsic to the concept of APL is the notion that people can be assessed without regard for any particular learning or training programme. As part of the assessment process, the focus is on *what* an individual has learned, not the time, place, or method of learning, or even the motivation of the learner.

Essentially assessment reflects four basic processes:

- *identifying* what an individual knows and can do;
- *equating* those skills and knowledge with specific standards, course or qualification requirements;
- *assessing* the individual against those standards or requirements; and
- *crediting* the learner in the appropriate manner.

It is the systematic approach to each of these that ensures a sound and equitable assessment programme: one that recognises the almost infinite way people learn and the diverse methods by which they can actually prove what they know and can do.

APL: *who benefits?*

Research over the past 20 years has provided significant evidence of the benefits of APL to both individuals and organisations. Individuals benefit in a variety of ways from the assessment process. Specifically, as an outcome of the recognition of what has been learnt, it enables them to:

1. build on their experiences and not have to relearn what they already know and can do;
2. shorten the time required to complete formal qualifications;
3. focus on their own development and training needs;
4. enhance their self-confidence as learners;
5. recognise the value of their accomplishments; and
6. often save time and money in reaching new goals.

Significantly, APL also appears to serve as a powerful motivator for individuals to seek new learning opportunities and complete recognised qualifications. Both in the UK and in North America there is growing evidence that adults completing the process grow more self-aware, are willing to take greater responsibility for their own development and have changed – generally more positive – attitudes about educational and training organisations. Even for those who already are self-confident, the process seems to lead to more focused learning and clearer goal setting.

In quite a different vein, APL helps people to earn needed qualifications more expediently. These qualifications, whether they be National Vocational Qualifications in Britain (NVQs) or diplomas in Canada or degrees in the USA, often enable people to re-enter the job market, explore new career paths, or seek promotions within their existing organisations. In each case, the qualification represents a valuable tool for empowering individuals and enabling them to move more readily in their chosen directions – directions which often mean that more effective use is made of the individual's skills and knowledge, leading to greater job and personal satisfaction.

Organisations also gain from the introduction of flexible assessment opportunities. They find they can:

1. maximise the effective use of their educational and training resources;
2. better meet the needs of individual clients, students or employees;
3. motivate their clients or employees to participate more willingly in, and to complete, the programmes;
4. provide equal opportunities to a greater range of clients; and
5. integrate assessment with ongoing services or programmes.

Competence-based assessment practices that embrace the basic concepts of APL can be used by organisations for any number of purposes, for example: as a diagnostic tool to identify an individual's strengths or limitations at the beginning of an education or training programme; to monitor progress against known standards or expectations (whether in education, training or work); or to grant credit towards a credential. Generally speaking, the concept of APL is found in organisations that are committed to the notion of learner-centredness, since the concept itself assumes that the learner is an active partner in the assessment and learning process. Colleges and universities using the principles of APL often see more highly motivated learners and higher retention and completion rates.

Who are the learners?

Learners include anyone who needs, wants or could benefit by receiving recognition or qualifications for his/her learning. The following examples of Jim, Sharon, Amina and Charles illustrate the diversity of backgrounds learners bring with them to the assessment process.

JIM

Jim is 35, married and has two children. He has worked for seven years as a computer salesman. He also has worked his way through an open-learning pack in selling and has participated in three on-the-job training workshops on presentation, negotiation and time-management skills.

Jim is also a member of the local Junior Chamber of Commerce, where he takes a lead in organising Chamber functions and events. He enjoys this challenge, which often involves his delegating tasks to his colleagues and managing a limited budget.

In Jim's current organisation internally advertised positions for managers often arise in various areas. Jim wants to move into one of these management positions; however, he realises that without any formal management qualification, he would be unlikely to get as far as the first interview. Jim knows that he has the experience necessary for the job, but just needs the opportunity to prove it. The assessment process will allow Jim to gain credit towards an NVQ Level 4 in management, which in turn will enable him to qualify for a job interview.

SHARON

Sharon left school after obtaining three A-levels in chemistry, physics and biology. She was always interested in chemistry and had obtained the necessary grades to embark on a degree in the subject. However, after leaving school she accepted a job as a technician in a chemistry laboratory at a nearby university. She has been working in this position for over four years.

Sharon's job as a technician is much wider than just preparing equipment and experiments. She has also been involved in giving demonstrations to undergraduates on liquid crystal displays and has read widely around the topic, which she finds fascinating. She has also been carrying out some research herself on liquid crystal displays, which she hopes to publish jointly with some of the research staff, who treat her as an equal and

7

respect both her interest and enthusiasm for the field, neither of which is a necessary requirement of her job.

Often research staff with whom she works advertise for research assistants. Sharon now wants to move into research full-time and feels she has the necessary experience to take on one of these jobs. However, university admission procedures stipulate that a degree is necessary for research positions. Sharon does not want to leave her technician job to study for a three-year degree. Not only does she need the money, she wants to keep in touch with ongoing research. APL will enable Sharon to gain credit for a large part of the degree programme and obtain her degree in a time-shortened period while still retaining her current job.

AMINA

Amina is 29 years old and has been working as a cook in her father's speciality restaurant since leaving school. She has never had any formal training in catering, but has practically run her father's restaurant during recent years. She learned everything about catering from her father and from on-the-job experience.

The restaurant is very popular with locals and appears in a number of good food guides. Unfortunately, Amina's father is getting old and is no longer interested in running the restaurant. Amina herself has enjoyed working in the restaurant but soon will be getting married and leaving her family home. Recently she has been applying for jobs in catering closer to where she intends to live. However, Amina has found that despite her experience, most modern restaurants require a catering qualification before hiring anyone. Obviously, Amina does not want, nor does she have the time, to go to college to relearn what she already knows. She has heard about S/NVQs in food preparation and thinks this may be what she needs. The assessment process would enable Amina to acquire a catering qualification and therefore allow her career to progress much more quickly.

CHARLES

Charles is 31 and single. Immediately after finishing school with few qualifications, he joined the navy. He spent five years in the service where he had the opportunity to visit many fascinating places throughout the world. Often, on shore-leave he would make a point of visiting places off the beaten track and away from the commercial ports. He kept a diary of what he encountered on his travels, noting peculiar features of the landscape and customs of local inhabitants.

On board ship, Charles spent his spare time reading books and local literature on the places he had visited. When not reading, he would be writing his diary on his thoughts and perceptions. Through his time in the navy Charles learned a lot about cultural differences and the diversity of local customs and rituals.

After completing his time, Charles worked for short periods in various jobs, but found it hard to find one which matched the excitement of the navy. One Sunday, he read an advertisement in a newspaper for volunteers to embark on a three-month field trip in the African rainforests. The organisers of the trip were investigating the detrimental effects felling of the rainforests was having on the African tribes. Charles saw this as a great opportunity to regain his interest in different cultures and as a route out of a mundane job. He applied to be a volunteer and after a number of interviews was accepted. He enjoyed the field trip immensely, during which he developed a good rapport and working relationship with the research team. He did not go home after the three months but continued working in Africa for a number of months, until the research team's funds ran out.

On returning home Charles managed to get a non-professional job with the research team he had been working with in Africa. Although this job was not highly paid, it was ideal for Charles. It gave him access to topical research and information on tribes throughout Africa and was not a 9-to-5 job. From time to time, opportunities also arose for Charles to visit Africa and other countries with the team.

Charles has begun thinking about the possibilities of obtaining a degree, particularly as all his colleagues at work have one. He believes that obtaining a university degree in anthropology, while not essential for his career, would give him a deep sense of personal satisfaction and might enable him to gain a greater level of independence in his organisation. He would like to use APL to earn as much credit for his prior learning as possible.

As exemplified by these four people, adult learners identify many reasons for seeking recognition and credit for their prior learning. For each, however, it brings the promise of greater personal and/or professional satisfaction.

Where did APL come from?

The basic premise of APL – that people learn by doing – has been around for centuries. There are many deep traditions of experiential learning easily recognised, from the writings of many Greek philosophers right through to the work of later philosophers such as John Locke, John Stuart Mill and others. In the context of the twentieth century, thinkers such as Jean Piaget, John Dewey, Kurt Lewin and David Kolb have each stressed the critical importance of experiential learning to human growth and development.

It is also possible to analyse a number of social movements to understand the origins of APL. For example, during the Middle Ages, the guild system required that the master determine when an apprentice was ready to move on to journeyman status and the journeyman on to master status. To no small extent this was a type of assessment and accreditation of prior learning.

From quite a different point of view, medical students are required to serve a period of internship before becoming professional doctors. These internships provide the experiential learning opportunities that reading books and attending lectures cannot and are viewed as essential to the development of the competent doctor.

Similarly, classroom teachers the world over also provide experiential learning opportunities. It is difficult to imagine any biology, music or computer programing course not containing a laboratory or action-learning experience. The belief that experiential learning is intrinsic to the development of any competent biologist, musician or computer programer (to provide but a few examples) is unquestioned in our modern training and educational world.

So if we believe that experiential learning is so critical to human experience and so deeply embedded in many of our current traditions, what is so unique about APL? Simply answered, APL forces us to recognise that *any* experience, whether formal or informal (and maybe even accidental!), may provide a powerful learning opportunity for an individual and that, with proper assessment, the outcomes of that learning experience can be formally recognised and credited.

The current APL movement developed in the USA during the late 1960s and 1970s. It was originally conceived as a research project at the Educational Testing Service in Princeton, New Jersey (CAEL, 1975). There were three basic questions to be investigated during the three-year study period:

1. Is it possible to equate non-college learning with that offered in traditional college curricula?
2. If it is possible, can assessment techniques other than paper-and-pencil tests be used to evaluate the outcomes of this learning?
3. If such a system proves feasible, would it be possible to integrate the ensuing model in current educational programmes?

This project, known as the Cooperative Assessment of Experiential Learning Project, involved ten colleges and universities. Outcomes of the project demonstrated that:

1. It was possible to equate non-college learning with that of traditional college curricula.
2. It was feasible to use a wide variety of evidence in conducting valid and reliable assessments.
3. The emerging process could well be embedded in existing educational programmes and was of particular use with

11

adults who were entering for the first time or returning to college or university with rich and varied experiential learning.

Today more than 1200 colleges and universities in the USA offer assessment and accreditation of prior learning programmes with a growing number emerging in the UK, Canada, Australia and New Zealand. In addition, greater numbers of employers are becoming involved in the work, most often fostering APL through joint ventures with a wide range of educational or training providers. The Council for Adult and Experiential Learning (CAEL), a leading national organisation in the USA, is actively engaged in promoting these joint ventures to bring APL and other educational and training programmes to people in the work place.

The development of APL in Britain

The assessment of prior experiential learning (APEL) was introduced in Britain in the 1980s largely as an outgrowth of on-going work in the USA. In 1980 the US-based Kellogg Foundation offered CAEL $25,000 (Gamson, 1989) to develop a British/American Scholars Exchange Programme. Through this programme a wide range of UK educators and policy makers visited American institutions that were advocating or implementing APL. Under the leadership of Norman Evans, director of the Learning from Experience Trust, a number of APEL projects were developed, primarily in higher education and most often for purposes of access to higher education by adults. Unlike the work that followed in the latter half of the 1980s, these early projects were not based on standards of competence or even learning outcomes. Rather they used profiling systems that provided evidence of both the need for such a service and a useful methodology that could be applied in a variety of higher education contexts.

This early APEL work coincided with a number of other

developments, namely the government's call for a more flexible, adaptable workforce; training programmes that were more responsive to the needs of employers *and* individuals; greater access to education and training for greater numbers of people, and so forth.

As far back as 1981 the Manpower Services Commission (MSC)* published a far-sighted review of vocational education and training in the UK called *A New Training Initiative* (HMSO, 1981). This stated the problem in unequivocal terms and provided a mandate:

> Britain needs a flexible, adaptable work force to cope with the uncertainties which cloud the future. The technological revolution and the need to become more competitive present real challenges for as far ahead as we can see. Markets and prices for products, processes and services will continue to fluctuate. Firms and individuals must either adapt to change or become its victims.

Developments in Scotland also contributed to and provided a framework for offering APL. Growing out of a decade-long interest in criterion-referenced assessment, in 1983 the Scottish Education Department announced an intention to convert the further education craft and technician education curriculum to a criterion-referenced format based on clear and explicit learning outcome statements. In implementing this Action Plan, as it was called, a decision was also taken to adopt a modular structure, replacing qualifications acquired by end-of-course examinations with a structure that typically replaced one year's curriculum with 20 modules.

At an early stage in the development, it was realised that if the

---

* While the MSC was a quasi-autonomous organisation, it was staffed by civil servants within the Employment Department. With the demise of the Commission in 1988, the functions and staff were assimilated back into the Employment Department. In 1996 the Employment Department was integrated with the Department of Education to become the Department for Education and Employment.

desired learning was expressed in clear and explicit criterion-referenced learning outcome format, learners could be assessed against the expected outcomes as soon as it was apparent that they had met the standards. Achievement of credit would no longer be tied to a fixed period of study. Indeed it was now possible to be assessed against the learning outcomes without attending a single class. Scotland had essentially found its own way to APL.

The 1986 White Paper *Working Together – Education and Training* (DE, 1986) lay further groundwork for the introduction of APL and the competence-based assessment system that followed: 'Qualifications and standards are not luxuries. They are necessities, central to securing a competent and adaptable workforce. Economic performance and individual job satisfaction both depend on maintaining and improving standards of competence'.

This same White Paper established the National Council for Vocational Qualifications (NCVQ) which was to take the lead in the reform of vocational qualifications which were to be based on nationally recognised standards of competence.

NCVQ also expressed a commitment to a unit-based structure. It came to the same conclusions regarding the potential of APL as had been reached in Scotland two years earlier. In 1987 the MSC (now the Department for Education and Employment) first mounted an exploratory study and then two major feasibility projects to investigate the potential of applying APL processes to National Vocational Qualifications (S/NVQs) and also, in Scotland, National Certificate modules.

Outcomes of the feasibility studies

As a result of these major feasibility studies, NCVQ, Scottish Vocational Education Council (SCOTVEC) and a number of the major awarding bodies endorsed the concept of APL and established policies and recommended implementation procedures. These organisations, along with the participating further education colleges, identified the key features of a sound APL service. These included:

1. A commitment by the organisation to establish a clear policy for the recognition, assessment and accreditation of prior learning.
2. A concrete plan to integrate APL with other educational and training services.
3. A strong commitment to staff development and on-going team building throughout the organisation.
4. Trained advisors and assessors.
5. A named person responsible for the management of the APL service.
6. A clear marketing strategy.
7. Modular instruction or access to alternative learning resources for all candidates.
8. A commitment to offer a range of assessment-on-demand services.

In addition, the feasibility studies provided the basis for a number of other projects, many funded by the Employment Department. Each was designed to investigate APL in different contexts and for different groups of people. It is worth noting a number of these projects to understand the full scale and impact APL is having on training and education in the UK. The 1990 Employment Department publication *Accreditation of Prior Learning: A Training Agency Perspective*, gives a full reference to these projects (ED, 1990).

During the 1990s, as the use of S/NVQs began to grow, trainers, educators and employers began to understand more about the nature of competence-based assessment. Increasingly people saw that the concept of APL was an integral part of the emerging assessment system. The lessons learned from the early APL work helped to better inform practitioners and policy makers alike, as they worked to ensure the quality and cost effectiveness of the S/NVQ system.

Occupational developments

Management

The Confederation of British Industry (CBI), the Foundation for Management Education (FME) and the British Institute of Management (BIM) with government support established a national organisation to:

1. develop a coherent Code of Practice to foster better training for managers;
2. develop national standards of competence for managers; and
3. promote the individual development of British managers.

This organisation is called the National Forum for Management Education and Development (NFMED). Its operational arm is the Management Charter Initiative (MCI) which is supported by a membership of more than 800 employers, representing 7.5 million employees, or about one quarter of the UK workforce.

As part of its work, the MCI learned that very few British managers over 35 years of age have had *any* formal management training or development. They also learned that most managers, regardless of age, do not *expect* to receive any management education or training. Although many managers do have some sort of formal qualifications, these are most often in professional areas such as accounting, engineering, chemistry, or at craft and technician level. Very few have qualifications reflecting what they do as managers (Tjok-a-Tam, 1991).

In conjunction with the development of national standards, a major APL project, supported by the Employment Department, was launched in 1989. It was designed to help managers:

1. recognise their strengths *and* weaknesses;
2. receive formal recognition towards national management qualifications; and
3. take greater responsibility for their own development and education as managers.

Working with a range of providers including further and higher education institutions, management development specialists (both schools and independent firms and associations), two large employers (British Gas and British Rail) and the BIM, more than 400 experienced managers completed the APL process in a nine-month period. Almost all earned credit towards a recognised management qualification; some were able to earn the full award.

As an outcome of the success of this project, the concept of APL was integrated with all of MCI's on-going initiatives under the banner of 'Crediting Competence'. Managers throughout the UK are now able to have their skills and knowledge – competence – assessed and recognised in the form of credit towards national qualifications. MCI staff and members have found that identifying, gathering and generating evidence against the standards in the form of a portfolio serves as a valuable learning tool for managers from all backgrounds and organisations. Since the early APL work, greater numbers of managers have sought to learn and develop to meet the standards, earn the qualification and become more responsible for their own training and development.

Other vocational areas
Candidates coming forward for NVQs have been able to use evidence of their past achievements in occupational areas as diverse as customer service, hotel and catering, computing, administration, care, horticulture and automotive technology. Today more than a million S/NVQs have been awarded, many of which have been achieved in employer organisations, not just in education and training organisations. This powerful uptake of NVQs in the workplace has meant an increasing awareness of the true meaning of 'diverse evidence' and the notion that people can – and should – receive accreditation for what they know and can do wherever and whenever it is learned.

The use of evidence from prior achievements within these areas has served to motivate many competent people who previously had little or no regard for formal educational

17

programmes to seek qualifications *and* new learning. It also has enabled people to value what they know and can do and, perhaps most importantly, it has demonstrated to individuals that they *have* and *can* learn. It is perhaps a sad commentary that so many intelligent, competent people were either rejected by traditional educational programmes or felt education simply had nothing to offer them. It is these people who initially come to APL cautiously but who often reap the most benefit.

The impact on user organisations themselves has been significant. They have had to address new issues related to admissions, placement, assessment, staff development, staff roles and organisational structure. Once a college, for example, knows the strengths of its incoming or potential students, they are able to provide learning opportunities that encourage the students to progress in new ways, not just take courses they don't actually need. Both employers and colleges have found that it no longer makes sense simply to send an individual on a two-year course in business studies, for example, when college staff (and the employer!) are already convinced that the candidate knows and can demonstrate most of the curriculum.

Underemployed and unemployed people
The diagnostic aspects of competence-based or flexible assessment systems are also being applied with some success with underemployed and unemployed people. The theory is that if we can help people identify what they already know and can do, it may be easier to design and provide more meaningful learning opportunities for them.

Many of the basic principles of APL can be effectively applied during initial assessments and in conjunction with other forms of psychometric and skills testing. Significantly, in Britain, North America and elsewhere, underemployed and unemployed people report how much they value the opportunity to identify and reflect on all they know and can do, whether or not they achieve a qualification. Not surprisingly, improved self-confidence, so necessary to breaking the cycle of underemployment or unemployment, has been a natural outcome for many people completing the process as part of 'returning to learning' programmes.

Training and Enterprise Councils
'Training and Enterprise Councils (TECs) have been created to unlock the potential of individuals, companies and communities across England and Wales' (ED,1991). One of their main aims is to raise the local skills base and spur business growth. They are directed by top business and community leaders with government funding, although it is expected that they will ultimately be able to generate a large percentage of their own income. Currently there are 81 TECs in England and Wales and another 13 Learning and Enterprise Companies (LECs) in Scotland.

One of the TECs' current priorities is to enable as many people as possible to obtain National Vocational Qualifications. Between 1990 and 1995 more than 50 TECs participated in the Access to Assessment Initiative (AAI), a national effort designed to systematically establish networks of assessors, increase employer involvement, and offer increasing support services to individuals wanting to achieve NVQs. Through AAI, TECs helped foster a wide range of partnerships and consortia arrangements that provided greater access and administrative ease to new assessment opportunities for individuals both in and out of employment.

Establishing these local competence-based assessment options has enabled colleges, employers, professional organisations and others to become more actively involved in assisting individuals to recognise and draw on all they know and can do to achieve NVQs. The Skills for Small Business initiative is building on some of the lessons learned from AAI by providing funding and expertise to small employers who also wish to introduce NVQs and develop their own assessors, in order to provide flexible assessment opportunities for their employees. All of these efforts have embedded the concept of APL in an effort to maximise the learning options and benefits of competence-based assessment to individuals throughout the nation.

Summary

The concept of APL, regardless of the terms used to describe it, is based on long-accepted theories and principles of experiential learning. The concept is intrinsic to the notions of competence-based assessment and flexible assessment. It recognises that what people know and can do is of value, regardless of how, why or when they learned it. Competence-based or flexible assessment systems actively encourage people to identify what they know and can do and become more active, focused learners. These systems are of significant benefit to both individuals and organisations. Stemming from early work in the USA, the movement has developed in several different ways in Britain and indeed continues to develop in unique ways in New Zealand, Canada, Australia and elsewhere.

In the USA, APL developed largely in the context of higher education and for purposes of credit. In Britain it was originally introduced as an alternative route to higher education for adults. But now, as a fundamental element of the competence-based S/NVQ system, it is being applied with a wide range of candidates in diverse settings and organisations across the nation.

Chapter 2

Roles and Responsibilities in Delivering Flexible Assessment Services

The implementation of flexible assessment services requires the involvement of many different kinds of people who bring to the process a wide range of professional skills and knowledge. It also requires that people work effectively not just as isolated individuals but as a team. This chapter reviews the various functions required to deliver flexible assessment services. But before describing these, it is important to understand the basic model itself.

The learner-centred assessment model

The basic learner-centred assessment model contains six stages, each having a set of specific objectives and activities (see Figure 2.1). While focused on assessment, however, this process cannot be understood or applied outside the context of learning and development. Assessment itself *is* a dynamic learning process – one that requires the learner to assume considerable responsibility for the outcomes. It is dependent on the learner's own self-assessment and commitment to the process. As such, this model reflects a dramatic shift in philosophy from an

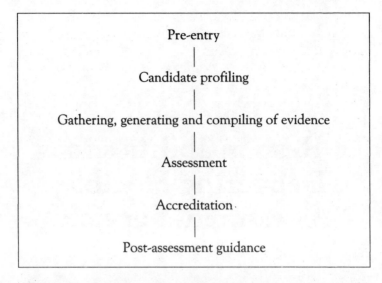

Figure 2.1 *The six stages of the learner-centred assessment model*

externally controlled assessment process to one that includes the learner as an essential and active partner.

This model, with some variation, has been adapted across training, education and employment contexts in an effort to foster more active learning, greater participation in the learning and assessment process, and increased confidence in individuals.

Stage 1: Pre-entry

During the pre-entry stage of this model, the organisation providing the service disseminates information to attract potential candidates. In colleges, this generally means that the institution gives insight into the process and in most cases links the service to others on offer. The primary objective of this stage is to give candidates adequate information to decide whether or not they wish to undergo the process.

Pre-entry activities in colleges and universities include distributing brochures, producing press releases, meeting with groups of employers or any of a whole range of other strategies that are used to market services and products and disseminate information. For employers this generally means letting employees know about the learning and development opportunities available, and promoting the idea of individual responsibility in achieving learning goals. Many companies promote this idea through company newsletters, group meetings or seminars involving external providers. Sometimes, of course, education and training providers work closely with employers, each using different techniques and strategies to convey comparable messages to prospective candidates. Such collaboration can be highly beneficial for all concerned.

Stage 2: Candidate profiling

During this stage, candidates reflect on their experiences and accomplishments and begin to develop a profile of what they know and can do. It is also during this stage that candidates clarify their expectations in seeking recognition of their learning and equate what they know and can do with the standards or learning outcomes of a particular programme or qualification.

There are several activities that may occur during this stage to help candidates develop their profiles.

1. Working individually, candidates may complete a written or computer-generated self-assessment. Most often, checklists related to specific standards or learning outcomes form the basis for this self-assessment.
2. Candidates may also prepare a written description or personal report of what they know and can do across many different areas of accomplishment, and later compare this profile to the standards or learning outcomes in which they wish to receive recognition.
3. In some situations candidates may undergo an interview with a trained advisor to develop the necessary profile. In helping the candidate the advisor may use one or more

checklists to help the candidate identify his or her areas of competence.

4. In still other situations, candidates may work in small groups to develop their individual profiles. This approach may be particularly useful in employer contexts.

Since a strong candidate profile is critical to the success of the assessment process, it is important for the providers of assessment to have clear and distinct ways of supporting candidates through the process. The clearer candidates are about their own strengths and how they relate to the standards or learning outcomes, the easier it is for them to collect or generate the evidence they need.

Also during this stage, candidates need to receive information and guidance on the range of acceptable evidence needed to support their claims to credit. This includes receiving information on current assessment techniques that also may be applied, eg demonstration, oral or written questioning, etc. As an outcome of this stage candidates should have a clear idea of their own strengths and limitations, their goals, the nature of diverse evidence, and the type of support that will be available to them throughout the process.

Stage 3: Gathering, generating and compiling of evidence

During this stage, candidates identify how they can best prove their competence or claim to credit and begin to collect and/or generate the necessary evidence. Their task is to make sure they have sufficient and valid evidence to prove they really know and can do what they claim. The standards or learning outcomes serve as their guide. This stage is fundamental to the learning and development of the individual. Although the candidate may be identifying and generating evidence to meet the assessment criteria, he or she is actually involved in an intense process of reflection and self assessment – essential to effective learning.

During this stage, candidates undertake a range of activities:

24

- they may prepare a personal profile or narrative statement;
- they may need to write to past or current employers for 'letters of validation' concerning their performance in the work place;
- they may need to gather from their place of work the products they have made or contributed to; and
- as part of the continuous learning process, they may also need to generate new evidence to supplement the other forms of available evidence.

Once gathered or generated, the evidence is then compiled and prepared for presentation. Most often this is in the form of a 'portfolio' or bound folder. However, not all evidence will be paper and many candidates will not have any physical evidence. Some candidates will be observed at work or in simulations and will not need to generate any additional evidence. Being observed generating the evidence becomes the assessment process itself! This is particularly true in workplace environments.

During this stage, candidates who have prepared narrative statements and/or generated physical evidence, prepare themselves for the next stage in the assessment process. The assessing organisation usually provides a range of services to help candidates prepare themselves. Written guidelines, videos, group workshops and one-to-one discussions – either in person, on the telephone, or through e-mail – are all effective strategies.

Stage 4: Assessment

This stage is composed of several mini-stages.

1. If a candidate has prepared a narrative statement and collected together physical evidence in the form of a portfolio, the assessor's first job is systematically to review the portfolio for completeness. He or she must be sure that the evidence relates to the standards or learning outcomes being claimed by the candidate and that there are no gaps in the evidence.

2. The assessor then needs to decide whether the evidence presented is valid and sufficient; that it provides full and ample proof that the standards or learning outcomes have been met.

3. If the assessor believes the evidence is valid and sufficient, then no further assessment would be required and the assessor could record the outcome, recommending credit or some other form of recognition. If the assessor believes that the evidence is *not* valid or sufficient, however, he or she will need to develop an assessment plan in order to help the candidate generate further evidence.

4. Once the assessment plan is in place, it needs to be communicated to and agreed with the candidate. Assuming the candidate agrees, final arrangements for the assessment can be made.

5. The assessor then assesses the candidate using one or more different methods of assessment.

6. The assessor provides feedback to the candidate.

7. Lastly, the assessor records the outcomes of the assessment and transmits it to the appropriate administrative or academic office.

Stage 5: Accreditation

Depending on the context in which this model of assessment is being applied, this stage will require action by the designated office actually responsible for awarding the credit or recognising the positive outcomes of the assessment. For example, within the context of further education in the UK, the national awarding bodies actually credit the candidate. Within the university context, however, it is the institution itself.

Stage 6: Post-assessment guidance

This final stage of the model underscores the developmental nature of the assessment process. After assessment (and hopefully accreditation), candidates need to reflect on what they have achieved and review how their accomplishments relate to their initial expectations and goals. For many candidates this final stage helps to integrate what has been learned during the process with the candidate's overall personal and professional targets. It also serves to enhance the candidate's self-confidence and often motivates him or her to seek new learning and development goals.

Usually it is the trained advisor who provides this post-assessment guidance. In many programmes, it is also the advisor who gathers candidate feedback on the process, thereby providing the organisation with regular and on-going formative evaluation information.

Functions and roles of staff

Functions

For each of the six stages outlined above, there are many broad functions that need to be carried out to run a successful learner-centred assessment programme. These include:

- Marketing
- Informing
- Advising
- Advocating
- Setting standards
- Assessing
- Keeping records
- Providing feedback
- Evaluating
- Facilitating learning
- Managing

Who actually performs these functions will vary from one institution to the next, but it is essential that an organisation determine the nature of each required function in its own context. An organisation uncertain about these functions will be unable to identify effectively the most appropriate people to carry out the various roles and responsibilities needed to introduce and sustain the assessment process.

Many of the functions cited above are offered primarily by mentors, advisors and assessors and these are described in detail in subsequent chapters. What follows, however, is a brief description of some of the key functions provided by others within an organisation which are also needed to implement a viable assessment service, namely, marketing, informing, setting standards (or learner outcomes), keeping records, facilitating learning and managing.

Marketing

Not so many years ago, colleges and universities rejected the concept of marketing. They may have 'disseminated' information, 'recruited' students, 'lobbied' for more money, but certainly did not undertake marketing – that was something only business and industry did! Now, of course, most organisations, whether in the public or private sector, market their goods and services – academic and training providers included.

On one level marketing learner-centred and flexible assessment services is no different from marketing any other service. The range of marketing strategies may well be the same. Brochures, posters, newspaper articles and advertisements, public presentations and so forth are all useful possibilities. Most organisations will find that marketing flexible learning and development opportunities will be far more effective than marketing flexible assessment services alone. Consistent with good practice in other contexts, organisations should use simple, jargon-free language that can be readily understood by potential candidates.

Expectations
Many assessment services during their development period make the mistake of promising more than they can deliver. They are so anxious to get people in the door that they create false hopes. Potential candidates come *expecting* that they will

automatically receive recognition or credit for what they can do and leave disappointed to have learned that (a) the process is not automatic or easy and (b) that in many instances what they know and can do is not appropriate or even relevant to the organisation offering the service. Marketing should encourage potential candidates but not mislead them.

Individuals or organisations?
In many flexible assessment programmes throughout the world, initial marketing efforts have been directed at individuals in the community. Some continue in this direction, although increasingly, as employers and others become more involved and committed to fostering better educated and trained workers, organisations offering flexible assessment services have focused their efforts on particularly receptive employers, unions or community agencies. This often leads to highly successful joint ventures in which both organisations gain considerably. Often, education and training providers find that they make better use of their resources if they work in this way with one or more organisations.

A separate or integrated service?
The notion of joint ventures raises yet another critical issue. Should the assessment service be promoted separately or along with the range of other services and programmes offered by the organisation? The answer depends on a number of factors:

1. Does the providing organisation have an overall policy for recognising and crediting learner achievements in all programme areas or only one or two vocational or academic disciplines?
2. Organisationally, *can* the assessment service be integrated? That is, have staff been given the necessary time and training to perform the various advising and assessing functions?
3. Are there clear links or progression points between the assessment services and other services and programmes within the organisation?

Historically, many colleges and training providers promoted APL as a separate entity. Although this approach served to raise awareness initially, prolonged separation of the assessment process from normal education and training provision marginalised the service, undermining the very purpose for which it was intended – to meet the needs of individual learners more flexibly and effectively. Learners themselves felt marginalised, reporting more than once that they felt like 'second-class' citizens participating in a 'second-class' process.

Increasingly APL – or flexible assessment – services have served as a catalyst for educational reform (Simosko, 1995). They continue to challenge some of the notions of traditional classroom instruction and are helping to focus attention on learning rather than teaching. They are enabling greater numbers of learners to be far more active in the learning, development and assessment process.

Informing

A second important function required of a flexible assessment service is providing information. All candidates need information to begin the process. But consider the range of information they need *during* the process. They need to know, for example:

1. how the process works at each stage;
2. the range of advice and support on offer;
3. roles and responsibilities of people to be involved;
4. the support materials available;
5. the schedule of workshops or briefing sessions;
6. the opening hours of any provider or assessment organisation;
7. the hours an advisor, assessor or mentor is available;
8. qualifications on offer;
9. fees;
10. time frames for each stage of the process;
11. how and when they will receive feedback;
12. how their credits (or other recognition) will be recorded;
13. opportunities for new learning and so forth.

They also need insight on the nature of acceptable evidence and assessment; and they need to know and be able to interpret the standards or learning outcomes on offer. Candidates and potential candidates are not the only ones who need information. Employers, union representatives, community service agencies, all of these need to know about flexible assessment. The function of 'informing', therefore, is another critical component in implementing a flexible service.

Who should do the informing?
Staff who have particular roles within the assessment process, namely advisors, assessors, training managers and S/NVQ coordinators, provide a lot of the information candidates require. Their roles are fully described in subsequent chapters. But they are not alone in helping candidates and others receive needed information about the service. All staff who serve as points of contact within an organisation or who represent the organisation in public forums can fulfil an informing function.

For example, it is often a well-trained receptionist, secretary or switchboard operator who can make the difference between a satisfied or complaining customer. People in such positions need to be trained as effectively as assessors: that is not to say that they need to know the *same* things, but they do need to be able to positively respond to enquiries, perhaps provide basic information about the service and offer the names of other institutional contacts. All too often the 'support' people within an organisation are ignored or minimally trained to respond to people's requests for information about a service. The results, as many organisations have learned the hard way, can be disastrous. For example, in the early days the college that failed to tell the switchboard operators what the letters 'APL' stood for. When a potential candidate telephoned and asked for the 'accreditation of prior learning' office, the switchboard office was emphatic that no such office existed!

In addition, it is not only 'support' people and those with specific roles and responsibilities in the assessment process who need to know details about the service. It is anyone within an

31

organisation who might be asked a question by a potential candidate, an employer or government policy maker, including senior managers. Everyone within an organisation – from senior manager to clerical assistant – should be able to provide the information requested or point the caller in the right direction. This is part of a Total Quality Management approach in employment contents, and reflects the truly learner-centred education and training organisation. An institution offering flexible assessment services needs to consider the many ways in which such information can best be provided and by whom.

Setting standards or learning outcomes

As is highlighted in Chapter 1, the UK government committed itself to the development of national occupational standards of competence. These national standards serve as the basis for National Vocational Qualifications (S/NVQs). These qualifications are offered through a number of national awarding bodies such as the City & Guilds of London Institute (CGLI) and the Business and Technology Education Council (BTEC). Learners work towards and obtain these new qualifications in school/ further/higher education, in employment, independently or some combination. (Please see Appendix for further details about S/NVQs.)

Since very few, if any other nations, have fully committed themselves to the development of standards in this way, most organisations wishing to offer a flexible assessment service need to set standards and learning outcomes. The process of setting standards becomes a prerequisite to offering a sound service. Whether the standards are called 'learning outcomes' or 'competence-based standards' or anything else, it is imperative that clear statements are in place and that all those involved in the assessment process – candidates, advisors, assessors, mentors and subsequent trainers or teachers – understand and can use the standards. It is impossible to assess candidates without an agreed standard by which to assess them. Keeping in mind that one of the key principles of the concept of APL is that it permits assessment *not linked to any particular learning or training programme*, it is essential that clear, assessable standards are developed.

Where there are no 'national' or externally defined standards, or learning outcomes, developing the standards is primarily the responsibility of subject specialists within a given institution or context, eg, a university department, a professional association, or industrial sector. Often these are the same people who serve as assessors. It is their job to determine the assessable outcomes of their work or training or academic programmes. Minimally they need to ask:

- 'What is it we expect our trainees, employees, or graduates to be able to do and know?' and
- 'To what standard and in what contexts do we expect them to be able to demonstrate that they have these skills and knowledge?'

An example may be helpful. In this example, taken from the Management 1 standards of the Management Charter Initiative, (MCI, 1991) in the UK, one activity expected of a competent manager is to:

Set and update work objectives for teams and individuals.

Although this statement sets out the activity – the element of competence, as it's termed – it does not specify the performance criteria against which the manager could be judged. The performance criteria attached to this activity are as follows:

1. Objectives are clear, accurate, and contain all relevant details including measures of performance.
2. Achievement of the objectives is practicable within the set period given other work commitments.
3. Objectives are explained in sufficient detail and in a manner, and at a level and pace appropriate to all the relevant individuals.

4. Objectives are updated regularly with the relevant individuals to take into account individual, team and organisational changes.
5. Individuals are encouraged to seek clarification of any areas of which they are unsure.

These standards also include specifications for knowledge and understanding, eg, principles and methods relating to establishing, defining and reviewing objectives and performance measures; defining and allocating responsibilities and authority. Also included is an indication of the range of conditions under which the performance should meet the standard and/or other delineation of range. Always the focus is on the outcomes: what we expect people to be able to know and do regardless of how they learned it.

Standards, it is important to add, can also be set for those capabilities sometimes called personal effectiveness traits. Many different models have already been derived covering a range of traits such as leadership, planning, and initiative (Astin *et al.*, 1986) and extending to statements like 'striving for improvement', 'making decisions', 'showing sensitivity to others', etc (Simosko, 1990). Here too, groups of professionals needed to decide what they meant by 'personal effectiveness' and once agreed they needed to develop criteria by which to judge the individuals under consideration.

Methods to set standards
There are many acceptable methods by which subject experts can work together to spell out what it is they expect learners to achieve and demonstrate. Some of the methods include DACUM, Delphi, functional analysis and others. All are based on gathering information about a particular occupation or field of study from those who are most knowledgeable. Some such as DACUM and functional analysis bring people together to work in groups. Others, such as Delphi, rely on survey methods in which participants learn the opinions of others but are not able to engage in discussion and debate. Each system has its strengths

and limitations. Professionals needing to develop standards would be wise to consult a range of source documents, most often available in reference libraries.

Further, those developing standards may be required or want to work with external organisations who can serve to 'validate' the usefulness or appropriateness of the standards – or any emerging qualifications based on those standards. In the UK, for example, the National Council for Vocational Qualifications serves to validate qualifications based on the standards developed by lead-industry bodies.

Keeping records

Good record-keeping is another key function of a successful assessment service, particularly in colleges and universities. It is a process many people take for granted. To implement flexible assessment effectively, however, most organisations find they need to reconsider their current procedures, sometimes making significant modifications or additions to accommodate the needs of candidates. Record-keeping takes place at each stage of the assessment process and involves not only the specific activities described below but also the organisation of a sound *system* for the storage and retrieval of records. This overall system needs to be evaluated regularly and modified to suit the changing needs of the organisation and the people who provide the service. This is as true for human resource development offices as it is for education and training providers.

Pre-entry

At the pre-entry phase most college-based assessment organisations try to maintain a list of people who write or telephone for information. They, like their employer counterparts, also maintain files of any potential candidates who attend briefing seminars or workshops. Since most potential candidates complete application forms, assessment centres must take care to collect the information that will be most useful in guiding the candidate through the system and have a systematic way of processing those application forms.

Profiling
At the second stage, profiling the candidate, there are additional record-keeping responsibilities. If advisors or mentors are working with candidates on a one-to-one basis, the outcomes of each session should be recorded and, following recommended procedures, shared and agreed with the candidate. The nature of the information recorded will vary, but at the very least it should specify:

1. the reasons the candidate is seeking the recognition;
2. any qualifications or portions of qualifications the candidate is seeking;
3. the actual 'profile' of the candidate, whether in checklist or sketched-out narrative form;
4. likely sources of evidence for the candidate; and
5. an agreed plan of action, eg, an assessment or learning contract or the date for the next meeting with the advisor, etc.

Gathering and generating evidence
While the candidate is actually gathering and generating his or her evidence during the third stage of the assessment process, the centre will want to record the outcomes of any telephone or written enquiries made by the candidate. In addition, if there are ongoing portfolio development workshops or other pre-assessing services being used, notes of a candidate's progress should also be recorded, always, of course, with the candidate's knowledge and approval. The reason for keeping such careful records of a candidate's progress is not to monitor the candidate *per se* but to provide as much helpful guidance and support as possible. This is especially true if more than one staff member is to be involved with the candidate prior to assessment. For example, a candidate may attend a weekly portfolio development workshop facilitated by one advisor but then telephone his or her own advisor at a later date for clarification about some

other matter. Careful records can ensure that candidates receive consistent information and, of course, from the centre's point of view, problem areas are more easily identified.

Assessment

The assessment stage requires the highest demands on the record-keeping function, whether the assessment takes place at work or in other settings:

1. Assessment plans must be carefully spelled out and agreed with the candidate.
2. The outcomes of each assessment must be carefully recorded.
3. Candidates must receive written and clear statements regarding the outcomes of their assessment.
4. Summary information required by third parties such as registrars or verifiers must be clear and comprehensive.
5. Administrative records need to be carefully completed to provide an accurate historical perspective of the candidate's assessment. For example, it would be essential for the record to indicate the date(s) of the assessment, the names of the assessor(s), the outcomes of the assessment, and the date and nature of the candidate's award.

Post-assessment guidance

This last stage of the process provides a good opportunity to review with candidates the records compiled on them during the assessment process, especially if careful notes have been kept about the candidates' original objectives. Often candidates are very pleasantly surprised to see how far they have come in meeting their initial target. Reviewing it with the advisor helps to reinforce and integrate all that the candidate has thus far achieved.

Most advisors also record any future plans the candidate may have set for him or herself, again to have a complete picture should the candidate return to the centre for additional support or assistance.

Facilitating learning

Although this book focuses on the assessment process, as pointed out in the preface, it is no longer possible to think about assessment as a stand-alone process. It is intrinsic to learning and development. Most people coming forward for assessment services do so because they are interested in their own development. Whether at work or in a college or university setting, the professionals who support the candidate must be knowledgeable about new learning opportunities and help individuals consider all of the learning and development options available to them.

In the UK and elsewhere, many learning opportunities have become modularized, allowing learners to dip in and out of the material they need. In addition, greater numbers of independent employers are modifying their training programmes to create more flexible and relevant learning opportunities, often linking these to the national standards or S/NVQs. All of this is helping to revolutionise the 'learning industry' and the roles and responsibilities of traditional trainers and educators.

In Britain, unit-based qualifications (S/NVQS) are making it easier for learners to link what they know and can do to the associated standards or learning outcomes. It is also making it easier for them to identify appropriate sources and types of evidence. In many respects this type of breakthrough in curriculum and qualification structure makes it easier for providing institutions and employers to help candidates actually achieve their goals with a minimum of red tape and bureaucratic waste.

It is important to add, however, that while open and flexible learning opportunities can provide exciting, self-paced opportunities for some people, there are those who require more structure and support. Many individuals lacking confidence in how to learn will benefit far more from more traditional approaches to learning.

Costs

Cost is another factor organisations need to consider as they investigate using distance or open learning options. One candidate in the field of information technology found that to obtain all the open learning packages he would have needed to 'top up' his learning, would have cost over £1000, when the actual traditional cost was well under £300! This particular candidate felt 'between the devil and the deep blue sea'. As he put it, 'On the one hand, I already know and can do a lot of what is required to meet the standards, but admittedly, not everything. But I'm also not prepared to give up my job to take the full day-time course or spend £1000 to get the little I need. Surely, there must be another option.'

For candidates like this one, a suitable option may well be 'flexible' or 'self-paced' workshops offered in the evenings or at the weekends. As some centres are demonstrating, properly designed, these workshops can allow large numbers of candidates to learn and progress at their own pace with support provided by peers and a limited number of paid professional tutors or trainers.

Centres offering flexible assessment may have a number of other ideas for providing learning opportunities. The important point is that the learning options need to be flexible, of real value to the candidate and appropriate to his or her unique learning needs.

Managing

Flexible assessment, like all other services and programmes, needs to be managed. And it needs to be managed by a named individual having a range of responsibilities and resources available. The person needs to have a staff to carry out the various functions required of the service, eg, advising, assessing, providing information, recording, etc, and a range of resources, eg, a physical location in which to offer the service, written support materials, etc.

The manager must be a very able manager of people because central to the success of any competence-based assessment service is a strong team. No one person can offer an effective assessment service. There must be a clear delineation of roles and responsibilities and the manager must facilitate an effective team approach to make the system work.

In employment contexts it will be particularly important to establish an S/NVQ or standards champion. Gaining the support of senior managers will be critical to the successful implementation of flexible learning and assessment services.

Total Quality Management (TQM)

There are many lessons to be learned from applying a TQM approach to the implementation of competence-based assessment services. At the heart of the TQM approach is a redefinition of the word 'quality'. Not so long ago, quality referred to luxury or high-cost items. Today, quality means putting the customer first, and that means:

- identifying who the customers are;
- finding out what they want; and
- providing that in the most cost effective and helpful way possible.

Applied to assessment, a centre must identify the potential users of the service, learn what they need and expect of the centre and then seek to provide all the necessary information, support, guidance, assessment and learning services that will satisfy the needs of the users.

To offer a full, viable assessment service, the centre must involve every employee in some way in the process, creating a strong team approach. Each team member should be trained to deliver some aspect(s) of the service. More importantly they should be pleasant to the customers and flexible in their approach. The centre will want to offer a range of flexible assessment and learning options for users (whether individual candidates or other organisations) and make sure each and every user, or potential user, feels welcome and valued. In addition, there must be visible signs that the senior management is fully committed to adequately resourcing and marketing the service and drawing on the ideas of the staff for continuous improve-ment. The case study provided below will highlight the way in which an organisation might use the concept of TQM to introduce competence-based assessment services. (Of course, for many employers, TQM was introduced long before S/NVQs!)

Case Study

A TQM approach to flexible assessment

- *Identifying customer requirements*

A local college with declining enrolments decided to approach a number of local companies to find out if they could be of service. Senior managers from both sectors set up a local forum in which mutual concerns could be discussed and issues addressed. At the very first meeting, some of the employers reported a series of problems:

1. They were having to retrain a number of recent graduates who lacked the necessary skills and knowledge to work effectively.
2. They were paying high fees for professional trainers to offer in-company courses similar to the ones offered by the college.
3. They were trying to recruit people who seemed to have the necessary skills and knowledge but no qualifications indicative of their performance.
4. Within each company there were middle managers and techni-cians who seemed unable or unwilling to progress or adapt within the company but who were too valued to be made redundant.

- *Satisfying customer needs*

The college management and staff set about developing possible strategies aimed at satisfying these customer needs. They came up with a number of ideas:

1. Auditing the curriculum with help from industry repre-sentatives.
2. Developing a new curriculum based on standards set by college staff and representatives of industry.

3. Introducing an assessment service which would allow people to earn credit for what they knew and could do.
4. Expanding the opening hours of the college so employees could make use of the college before and after work and at weekends.
5. Introducing open and distance learning options as well as flexible learning workshops or forums, some of which would be held on the company's premises.
6. Modifying admission procedures so that everyone has an opportunity to profile his or her strengths and interests before progressing on a new learning programme.
7. Developing a staff training programme for the college which would make each person more responsive to the needs of both external and internal customers.

● *Providing customer service*
The management of the college endorsed the idea of these changes and began working with a number of different teams whose objectives were:

1. to establish whether or not the college could provide these services, and
2. if they could, how they were to facilitate the necessary changes.

● *Commitment to training*
A major part of the implementation plan was a commitment to staff training on three levels:

1. an awareness programme of what total quality means in relation to self and customers;
2. advice on organisational changes that must take place in order to 'put the customer first'; and
3. specialist training for individuals in order that they could function within the new set up, eg, specific roles within the assessment service.

● *Measuring success*
The dramatic increase in enrolments was the most obvious short-term measure of success. The new enrolments came from three main areas:

1. Existing employees from local companies came on part-time courses which were *now* comparable with the courses being offered by in-company trainers.
2. New employees in many local companies, who had no formal qualifications but had experience, enrolled for and acquired qualifications through the college assessment service.
3. Learners from the local community were now able to enrol on courses due to the new flexible approach of the college, particularly with flexible assessment, which opened up many opportunities for the adult population.

Success of the TQM approach to flexible assessment was not only measured through the increase in enrolments. A much broader and longer-term effect was in relation to staff attitudes throughout the college. Every employee, from the switchboard operators to senior managers, had undergone some form of staff development or training. This not only increased people's sense of worth in the college but had a positive effect on the college's dealings with the public.

Many employers in Britain are also achieving the Investors in People (IIP) award. Achieving this provides a public statement of an organisation's commitment to developing its people. Introducing standards and helping employees achieve S/NVQs is an important component of that commitment to the development process. Assessment becomes an ongoing process as employees learn and develop. The case study below provides a useful illustration.

Case Study

IIP and flexible assessment

In order to stay competitive, a small, UK-based training company decided to work towards IIP. It had three primary reasons for doing so. It wanted to:

- demonstrate to potential customers that it was committed to fostering the development of every staff member;
- encourage all members of staff to stay up to date; and
- enhance the team approach to running the business.

It developed a mission statement collaboratively and looked at the short- and long-term goals of the company. It reviewed all jobs and tried to anticipate the career goals for each member of staff. As part of this review, all members of staff – including the managers – identified current and future NVQs they wanted to achieve. From this each staff member developed a personal learning plan.

In collaboration with a local training provider, each member of staff began to reflect on his or her strengths against the national standards and generate evidence in the areas in which they felt they were already competent. They used the management, administration and training and development standards to guide their work. While they generated evidence as part of their daily work, some of them also participated in 'top up' workshops offered by the local college. These workshops enabled them to develop in new areas and apply their achievements to their work.

Over the year-long period it took the company to achieve the IIP award, the staff observed that:

- they had learned more about one another's roles and were able to help and mentor each other in new ways;
- they improved their individual skills and became more effective in responding to customers;
- their communication with one another improved;
- their job satisfaction increased; and
- they felt they were far better able to meet the organisation's mission, cost-effectively and with improved customer satisfaction.

These two case studies, one drawn from TQM and another from IIP, serve to highlight how dramatically the concepts of APL (flexible assessment) have been used to meet customer needs, enhance business development and improve employee motivation. Other business development concepts, such as the Learning Organisation, may provide an equally valuable vehicle for demonstrating how flexible assessment and learning strategies can be integrated in broad human resource development plans.

Summary

The basic competence-based assessment model contains six stages, which are not necessarily discrete: pre-entry, candidate profiling, gathering and generating evidence, assessment, accreditation, and post-assessment guidance. Each one of the stages requires a number of people with different skills to carry out a wide range of functions, ranging from initial marketing to managing and evaluating the programme. Assessors, advisors, coordinators and all other involved staff have to work both individually and as part of a team in order to run a successful competence-based assessment programme.

Identifying and satisfying the needs of the customer is the cornerstone of Total Quality Management (TQM). If assessment is to be truly flexible and responsive to learner needs, it also must be about satisfying the needs of the customer. It is therefore clear that a TQM approach to assessment is an excellent starting point in planning and implementing a flexible assessment service.

Chapter 3

Advising, Mentoring, Supporting

Flexible assessment, as we have seen in Chapter 2, is a learner-centred service. It is designed to 'put the customer first' and help each candidate to meet his or her individual goals. All candidates, however, no matter how well motivated, require information, encouragement and advice as they progress through the process. Some do fine with a minimum of help and support, others require a lot of attention and creative mentoring.

In this chapter we will look at the role of the advisor in supporting and mentoring candidates through the assessment process. We identify the primary responsibilities of the advisor, describe effective ways of working with candidates, and offer some helpful hints in setting up a range of advising services.

In addition, we refer to the advising unit, D36, of the Training and Development Lead Body (TDLB) standards, now the responsibility of the Employment Occupational Standards Council (EOSC). The term TDLB will be used throughout to denote these units. (These standards are described further in the final chapter.)

Role of the advisor

The role of the advisor in flexible assessment is primarily that of mentor, a 'wise and trusted guide'. The advisor serves as the candidate's advocate and offers information, advice and guidance. In fulfilling this role the advisor's most essential purpose is to help empower candidates, thereby enabling them to assume increasing responsibility for themselves and to make sound decisions. The role as set out by the TDLB (D36) is to:

Advise and support candidates to identify prior achievements.
- Help the candidate to identify relevant achievements.
- Agree and review an action plan for achieving qualifications.
- Help the candidate to prepare and present evidence for assessment.

Reflecting

One of the primary outcomes of the second stage of the learner-centred assessment process is the development of a profile that portrays what a candidate knows and can do. Sometimes candidates are able to develop these profiles on their own using a variety of self-assessment tools, but most often they need some form of help or encouragement. For many candidates this help comes from the advisor, whose main task is to help the candidate reflect on experiences and accomplishments which will enable the candidate to develop a comprehensive profile of his or her strengths and abilities.

Many candidates come to the assessment process believing that they have very little 'creditable' learning. There is a tendency for them, especially those who are a bit unsure of themselves, to discount much of what they know and can do. It is the role of the advisor to help candidates 'lift the canopy' from their often limited self-perceptions and damning self-appraisals.

Advisors do this in many different ways. The more effective ones:

- gain the trust and confidence of the candidates;
- are active listeners;
- give useful and sensitive feedback;
- ask relevant questions;

47

- suggest new ways of seeing things; and
- link apparently disparate ideas or facts and offer these for the candidate's consideration;
- help candidates set realistic expectations;
- enable candidates to anticipate, monitor and value the learning process that is intrinsic to the assessment process.

The standards reflect this by indicating that as an outcome of competent advising:

- the candidate is encouraged to review all relevant experience;
- support and the way it is given encourages self-confidence and self-esteem in the candidates; and
- candidates are given accurate advice and appropriate encouragement to enable them to form realistic expectations for the value and relevance of prior achievements.

Active learners

Candidates also need to be encouraged to reflect on themselves *as learners*. Many adults acknowledge that they know and can do something but they will not readily admit to being *actively engaged in the learning process itself*. As they begin their assessment work, adults regularly view learning as a passive or unconscious function. How many advisors have asked a candidate, 'When and how did you learn to do that?' only to hear, 'Oh, I don't know. I guess I picked it up somewhere', or 'I think I just was lucky; someone showed me a thing or two,' or 'Everyone knows and can do that . . . nothing special about that!' The advisor has a unique opportunity to help the individual see him or herself as someone who has *control* over what has been or could be or will be learned. Giving the learner control is perhaps the most profound way of 'putting the customer first'.

As was pointed out in Chapter 1, much of what we all learn seems to be unconscious and many of the skills we possess are acquired seemingly accidentally. Yet on reflection, it is often possible to see that perhaps the process of learning was not as unconscious or as accidental as it seemed. When people really have an opportunity to review and consider how they have come to know or do something, they often see that circumstances, motivation and their relationships with others have each played a critical role in the acquisition of their skills and knowledge. They also come to see that to a very large degree they were actively involved in solving problems, making choices, allocating resources, etc at the very time they were 'accidentally' learning something.

Although flexible assessment is a tool used by a wide variety of people to receive formal recognition or credit for their skills, knowledge and abilities, it also serves as a valuable opportunity for personal development. It is important for advisors to be aware of this aspect of the process and to foster, as often as possible, the notion of 'active learning'. Active learners are more inclined to take greater responsibility for themselves, to demonstrate a higher level of self-confidence and to value education and training. Surely these characteristics are central to the goals and activities of all professionals who are in the training or education business, particularly those charged with the role of advising, mentoring or supporting others.

Recent studies with employees have revealed that the very act of generating and gathering evidence to meet occupational standards promoted positive change and more active learning among employees. This in turn enabled the employees to contribute more effectively to the workplace and reduced training time away from work. Supervisors observed employees growing in self confidence as they worked towards the standards, and taking significant pride in their accomplishments. Advisors need actively to encourage and motivate individuals to move in these directions.

Advising, not telling

Advising requires each advisor to find the right balance between 'telling' and 'advising'. And indeed, it is often a delicate balance to find. The advisor who helps his or her candidates by telling them what to do may be very problem-centred. But often in focusing on the problem, the advisor excludes the candidates from the problem-solving process, thereby denying them the opportunity to take greater responsibility for themselves (De Board, 1989).

Advising in a competence-based assessment system requires the advisor to address the candidate's particular needs in gaining recognition for his or her achievements and to help the candidate to understand the details of the process. A significant part of the advisor's responsibility is to 'inform' the candidate, provide all of the current and accurate information the candidate needs, clarify the roles of the various people with whom the candidate will interact, describe the support services available and so forth. As described in the TDLB Standards, 'the candidate is given clear and accurate information about the reasons for, and methods of collecting and presenting evidence of, prior achievements'. In the context of flexible assessment, information is power.

It is also essential, of course, that the advisor addresses the unique problems or hurdles that confront the candidate and recognises that individuals will have different ways of solving problems, making decisions and learning from their own experiences. A competent advisor will get as many facts and details about the candidate as possible and, based on that information, develop a number of options and alternatives for the candidate to consider. This is especially true, for example, when candidates are trying to identify the various sources and types of evidence they might (or might not) be able to generate.

Mentoring, not protecting

As a mentor, the advisor must also encourage candidates to set out their own strategies and solutions to problems that emerge during the assessment process. Keeping in mind the 'wise and trusted guide' definition, the advisor must try to support the candidate to take full responsibility for his or her own actions and quietly withdraw to the background as the candidate gains self-confidence and a sense of purpose. It is the wise advisor, indeed, who lets go at the right time. (Increasingly, managers and supervisors are performing a mentoring function with their employees. This work can be extremely helpful in complementing the efforts of the advisor. And indeed, in some situations, the role of the advisor and workplace assessor are fulfilled by the same person.)

Flexible assessment advisors, however, like the mentor in Dante's *Divine Comedy*, also need to alert candidates to potential hazards and pitfalls. This is as much a part of the informing role as describing the role of the assessor or any other aspect of the process. As the mentor, the advisor should *want* the candidate to succeed with as little red tape and difficulty as possible. But the advisor also must remember that he or she cannot protect the candidate from making mistakes, feeling discouraged or not earning the recognition the candidate seeks. Ultimately, it is the candidate who is responsible for his or her own success or lack of it in gaining recognition or credit, not the advisor.

A resource, not a clinical counsellor

Serving as an assessment advisor is not always an easy role to assume. There is often a tendency for new advisors to want to get too involved in the particular circumstances of an individual's life, to rescue the candidate in some way. By listening to the life stories which often emerge as part of candidates' reflections, advisors are frequently moved by a deep and profound desire to help candidates out of what may be painful or dangerous life situations.

For many candidates, the assessment process offers a first-time opportunity to actually talk about themselves in detail with someone genuinely listening. Even though the main purpose of meeting with an assessment advisor is to help the candidates develop profiles that can be used to seek formal recognition or credit, it is inevitable that other details of the candidate's life also will emerge. For example, in describing how she came to own her own successful business, one woman painfully relived with her assessment advisor the family circumstances that led her into a period of dire economic poverty which forced her to completely alter her life. She began crying and had difficulty getting control of herself.

Using common sense, the assessment advisor got the woman a warm drink and some tissues and waited for her to regain her composure. The advisor then dealt with the situation in a kind and gentle way by acknowledging the pain the woman obviously was feeling and asking if she would like to continue the meeting or return for another appointment.

What the advisor *did not* attempt to do was delve into the woman's past, analyse her problems or offer therapeutic support. It may be that at a later date, if the opportunity presented itself or the matter arose again, the advisor might be able to let the woman know about a local counselling facility and leave the decision about whether to use it to the candidate herself. In this and other contexts, flexible assessment advisors serve as valuable resources to their candidates. Ideally they are familiar with local services and networks in their communities and can provide important information and referrals that will enable candidates to receive the assistance or information they might need – quite unrelated to the assessment process itself.

Advisors, however, are not therapeutic counsellors or psychotherapists. It is not their job to solve candidates' personal or psychological problems. Putting aside all the obvious ethical and legal implications, attempting to provide a psychological service, rather than one that is basically educational, could be extremely damaging to the candidates *and* their well-meaning advisors.

Many organisations find it beneficial to their candidates to establish formal relationships with other organisations in their local network. Such relationships can serve to clarify roles and responsibilities and reduce ambiguity and frustration for the candidates. In many employment sectors, employers are forming consortia and other arrangements to maximise support and assessment options for their employees. Working in such a collaborative environment enables advisors to make far more appropriate referrals, rather than trying to meet all the candidates' needs alone.

Supporting, not building false expectations

Advisors serve as the candidates' contact and support throughout the assessment process. Advisors, then, have yet another important responsibility: to support and motivate the candidate but not create false expectations that will set the candidate up for failure or disappointment. This requires another delicate balance.

Most experienced advisors quickly learn to be sensitive to the needs of their candidates and provide the type of support they need. For example, one advisor reported that every Monday morning she would receive a telephone call from one of her candidates. The candidate's purpose in calling was to tell her about the work he had completed on his portfolio over the weekend and to seek her approval for proceeding. The advisor said she was actually sorry when the candidate had completed his portfolio because his sense of enthusiasm and pride was often an inspiration to her, especially on Monday mornings! Clearly, for this candidate, the best support the advisor could provide was to (1) acknowledge and praise the candidate's progress, (2) respond to any questions he presented, and (3) offer encouragement for the next piece of work the candidate had to tackle.

By contrast, another candidate contacted the advisor infrequently and, when she did so, it generally was out of a sense of obligation. To the advisor, the candidate seemed demotivated and unable to focus on the work for any extended period of time. Over the course of several months her advisor was able to offer five different types of support:

- he arranged to meet with her individually on several occasions to discuss particular problems she was having;
- he arranged for her to join a 'portfolio development group' of others who were developing their portfolios;

53

- he asked to review her work in small segments to give her on-going feedback, rather than wait until she had completed her entire portfolio;
- he also helped her to develop a realistic schedule for completing her work (taking into consideration her home and work responsibilities); and
- lastly, he discussed her unique issues regarding evidence with the assessor in order to give her the best guidance he could as she gathered and developed the necessary documentation for her portfolio.

As these examples illustrate, candidates vary in the amount and nature of the support they require. Advisors often have difficult decisions to make regarding the time and other resources they can offer to any given candidate. Early on in their relationship with the candidate, advisors need to spell out as clearly as possible the parameters of the support on offer and control any tendency some candidates may have to misuse the options available. For example, many advisors set particular hours each week for receiving candidates' telephone enquiries. Candidates who are unwilling or unable to telephone during those hours need to be helped to find alternative ways of communicating with the advisor. Although flexible assessment is very much a candidate-centred service, advisors have the right and responsibility to control their time, resources and support in keeping with the best practices of their organisation and profession.

Providing facts and figures

The role of the advisor is complex and requires a good deal of creativity and sensitivity. It also requires knowledge of all the facts and figures associated with the process. It is the advisor who must know and convey the costs, fees, and timetable of the service. It is also the advisor who will need to identify the location and office hours of others the candidate will see during the process, eg, the assessors, the registrar, etc. And it is the advisor who will introduce the details of the entire process to the candidate and provide technical guidance on such matters as assessment alternatives. Lastly, it is also the advisor who will explain the range of support services and materials on offer. This is summarised by the TDLB standards as 'the candidate is given clear and accurate information about the reasons for and methods of collecting and presenting evidence of prior achievements'.

In most instances organisations prepare a lot of this information in written form. It can then be distributed to the candidate and reviewed as necessary with the advisor. For some candidates who have limited reading skills, of course, the advisor will need to provide the information orally. Increasingly, technology is also helping candidates learn about the assessment process.

Candidates will seek out advisors for all sorts of reasons, some related to the assessment process, some not. Often an advisor will have just the answer or information the candidate needs, but it is the wise advisor who recognises that he or she will not have all the answers all the time for all the candidates. And it is the *very* wise advisor – the one who puts the customer first – who sometimes guides the candidate in other, more appropriate directions.

Summary of advisor responsibilities

As may already be obvious, within this role, assessment advisors have many responsibilities. They must be able to:

- encourage people to clarify goals, identify obstacles or issues and develop strategies for overcoming them (D361c/D362b);
- help candidates reflect on their past experiences and identify their strengths and accomplishments (D361b/ D362d);
- assist candidates to develop a strong personal profile which is linked to the standards or course(s) against which the person wishes to be assessed (D362b/c);

- provide correct and adequate information which will enable candidates to make sound decisions (D361a);
- help candidates develop their portfolios of evidence and prepare for assessment (D363a/d);
- actively listen to candidates and provide appropriate feedback throughout the process (D361d/e/D363b);
- liaise with assessors and others on the assessment team (D363c); and
- maintain accurate records (D363e).

(The relevant performance criteria are shown after each bullet.)

The remainder of this chapter looks at how advisors can effectively meet all of these responsibilities for each candidate and do so in a calm, systematic and cost-effective way.

Effective ways of working with candidates

Most advisors find they need to develop a coherent framework or system for working with each candidate. This is the only way they can genuinely make sure that they provide a comparable service to all candidates and maintain necessary control of their own valuable time. The first part of this framework is often called the 'staged' or 'structured interview'. As the name suggests, there are several different stages or steps within this model which enable the advisor and the candidate to progress systematically during the profiling stage of the flexible assessment process and into the gathering of evidence stage.

The staged interview

The staged interview is generally divided into six distinct phases. These include:

1. Welcome and introduction.
2. Establishing the candidate's aims in seeking assessment.

3. Reflecting on the candidate's experience and accomplishments.
4. Linking the candidate profile to the recognition or qualifications sought.
5. Matching specific skills and knowledge to the standards or learning outcomes specified in the qualifications.
6. Developing an action plan or contract.

We will look in detail at each of these stages and describe the range of expected outcomes for each.

Stage 1: Welcome and introduction
As the name suggests, this stage often marks the real beginning of the assessment process for many candidates. It may be the first time the candidate meets his or her advisor individually. (In some centres, candidates may have the opportunity to attend a group briefing or orientation session at which they actually meet the advisors in a group situation.)

Although the words 'welcome' and 'introduction' seem simple enough, it is interesting to hear a group of professionals describe what they actually do during this stage. Good practice suggests that:

- candidates be greeted in such a way that allows them to know they were expected;
- advisors extend a smile, handshake and/or other informal greeting;
- advisors ask to be called by their first names; and
- advisors clarify with the candidate the name he or she wishes to be called.

It is essential that the candidate be encouraged to feel welcomed and that the environment seems well organised, pleasant and credible. Advisors should aim to create a friendly but business-like atmosphere. Some adults have reported feeling a bit intimidated at the beginning of the interview and then report how pleased they were to feel that they were dealing with a 'real person' who was taking them seriously. On the other hand, other adults have sometimes been put off by advisors who have tried a bit too hard to be friendly and establish instant rapport.

Clearly each advisor needs to use the words and mannerisms that best suit him or her. The outcome of this very brief, but critical, phase of the staged interview is to make the candidate feel comfortable and ready to begin.

Stage 2: Establishing the candidate's aims in seeking assessment
The length of time required for this phase of the interview will vary from programme to programme and from candidate to candidate. Some candidates come to the interview very clear about their aims in seeking credit or recognition, others may be quite vague. It is up to the advisor to make sure by the end of this stage that candidates have clear and realistic expectations of the process.

To get to this outcome, it may be necessary for advisors to confirm that candidates have adequate knowledge and understanding of the assessment process itself. If the candidates have attended an orientation session or have received, read and understood written or computerised materials about the process, this may be a relatively simple matter. Some candidates, however, will need to have the advisor review the process in some detail before they can actually develop a clear picture for themselves. Organisations often produce written or other visual materials to help advisors explain the assessment process, sometimes in more than one language or sometimes geared to candidates with special needs, eg, large print or audio tape for candidates with limited vision.

Even when candidates seem to understand the assessment process, some advisors find it useful to summarise or review the process just to be sure the candidate has no questions. They also highlight the role of the assessor and make sure the candidate is clear on the differences between 'advising' and 'assessing'. The advisor must make sure candidates realise that he or she is the 'advocate', not the 'gatekeeper' and that at the end of the process, it will be the assessor, not the advisor, who actually does the assessment.

Once the advisor is sure the candidate understands the process, it is important to check the candidate's aims and expectations, the basic purpose of this stage of the interview. To do this, advisors need to begin the questioning process and listen carefully to the candidate's responses. If the candidate seems to have unrealistic aims and cannot be helped by the process, the advisor needs to try to provide other information, if available, that may be more useful to the candidate.

However, if the candidate's aims are likely to be met by the centre's assessment process and the benefits to the candidate are quite obvious, the advisor will want to record the agreed aims and move on to stage three of the interview.

Before leaving this stage of the interview, however, it is important to add that most advisors in colleges or training organisations make extensive use of the candidate's application form which in many assessment services is completed and sent to the advisor well before the interview begins. The application form can provide basic information about the candidate's work and voluntary experience, his or her reasons for seeking credit or recognition and other details that the organisation and the advisors feel will be most useful to all concerned.

Clearly, as the advisor and the candidate begin their work together, the advisor should encourage the candidate to ask as many questions as may arise. Similarly, it is the advisor's responsibility to ask questions too to help clarify the candidate's expectations and his or her aims in seeking recognition.

Stage 3: Reflecting on the candidate's experience and accomplishments
During this stage the advisor must work with the candidate to identify those experiences and accomplishments most relevant to the candidate's aims. Again, the application form can provide the basis for many of the questions the advisor will want to ask. The candidate's responses will lead the advisor to ask others.

To encourage candidates' reflections, advisors generally use two types of questions: open- and closed-ended questions.

- An open-ended question requires the candidate to elucidate or develop his or her thoughts. For example, if the advisor said, 'I notice from your application form that you have had several different jobs in computing over the past five years', and then asked, 'What did you like or dislike about each one?', that would be an open-ended question. The candidate could respond and elaborate as he or she felt necessary.
- A closed-ended question requires the candidate to give a specific response. For example, if the advisor said, 'I notice from your application form that you also worked in the local hotel. Did you supervise staff there too?', then the candidate would be required to answer 'yes' or 'no'.

Examples of other open-ended questions include:

- How did you feel about that?
- Sounds interesting . . . tell me more . . . .
- Why did you decide to do that?

Examples of other closed-ended questions include:

- Did you use power tools?
- How often did you do that?
- How long ago did you complete that qualification?

Candidates will vary considerably in their ability to reflect and express themselves with the advisor. Advisors will generally find it necessary to use a wide variety of open- and closed-ended questions to help candidates develop their profiles. During this phase, it is essential that the advisor demonstrates good active listening skills so that each candidate is encouraged throughout the process. In summary, at this stage advisors will find that they need to:

- elicit information from the candidate, both general and specific;
- provide ongoing feedback;
- point out associations and linkages whenever possible; and
- help the candidate integrate or mould his or her reflections into a coherent profile.

Stage 4: Linking the candidate profile to the recognition or qualifications sought

This stage is essentially an extension of stage 3, during which candidates link their profiles to the qualifications or units of recognition on offer. Once the candidate and advisor agree the general direction in which the candidate wishes to go, the advisor must provide information about the various qualifications (or units) on offer that seem consistent with the candidate's personal aims and his or her objectives.

Candidates might begin by looking at the titles of qualifications or units in the areas of interest and from these select those that best reflect their accomplishments and competence. In higher education contexts candidates may need to see the descriptions or learning outcomes for the courses for which they are hoping to receive accreditation. In other UK contexts, they might review the S/NVQs in their areas.

It is important during this stage that the candidate receive as much support and help as possible. Advisors need to encourage the candidate's active involvement in linking his or her profile to the units or qualifications on offer. This is not always an easy activity for candidates to undertake. Often they are unsure of the standards of performance expected or of the language being used. The advisor should try to guide the candidate without being prescriptive.

Many organisations develop checklists – either paper or technology-based – to help candidates through this process. The checklists should reflect in easy-to-understand language the standards, learning outcomes or courses on offer.

Advisors must make sure that candidates have adequate time to complete this stage of the work. Sometimes candidates will want to take the checklists home to complete before resuming the interview with the advisor on another day. In workplace contexts, candidates may work with colleagues, their work team or manager to identify relevant units. (Sometimes employers will specify the units or qualifications they expect their employees to achieve.) In any event, the main outcome of this stage of the interview is the identification of the qualifications or units for which the candidate wishes to be assessed and receive accreditation.

Stage 5: Matching specific skills and knowledge to the standards or learning outcomes specified in the qualifications
During this stage candidates must complete two different activities:

1. They must begin to match their specific skills and knowledge to the requirements specified in the qualifications, units or courses for which they are seeking credit.
2. They must begin to identify possible sources of evidence that they can use to prove that they really do possess the skills and knowledge they claim.

Both of these steps require that the candidate take a closer look at the specifications on offer and receive information on the nature of acceptable evidence that could be used.

Once again, many advisors find it most helpful to use checklists at this point in the process. As in stage 3, candidates may wish to:

- complete the checklists with the advisor, colleague, work-team or manager;
- complete the checklists in a nearby room, after making a start with the advisor;
- take the checklists home to complete;
- use a computer data bank of checklists.

Advisors need to be prepared to describe to candidates the

nature of acceptable evidence that might be used in the candidate's portfolio so that, as they complete the checklists, they can begin to make notes regarding the evidence they have available, could acquire or generate. Once completed, these checklists serve as the basis for the candidate's final claims to credit.

Before moving on to stage 6, it is important to highlight the iterative nature of stages 3, 4 and 5. For any given candidate, these three stages may overlap or candidates may need to go back and forth between stages. For example, it is not unusual for a candidate to continue to add to or modify his or her profile (stage 3) as he or she works with the checklists presented in stages 4 and 5. Very often the checklists will suggest activities, accomplishments or skills that the candidate may have forgotten or dismissed as unimportant. Similarly, candidates frequently come to see that they know and can do a lot more than they originally thought and therefore often change their aims (or the qualifications) they are seeking.

Advisors need to be sensitive to the needs of each candidate and be willing to adapt the interview accordingly. Candidates progress through these three stages of the interview at their own rate and in their own manner. Some may have a very clear idea of how to work with checklists and compare themselves to the standards; others will need a lot of support. By using a staged interview approach, advisors will have a clear notion of the outcomes each candidate needs to achieve and a framework in which to offer the necessary help and support.

Stage 6: Developing an action plan or contract
This final stage of the interview brings the candidate and the advisor to a point of agreement about the work to follow. It allows the candidate the opportunity to commit to paper his or her plan to continue with the assessment process. It also provides the advisor with a document by which he or she can support and encourage the candidate.

An action or assessment plan is a simple form completed by the candidate and signed by the advisor that specifies what the candidate intends to do next. It is a fluid document that helps the candidate and the advisor monitor progress. It can be updated or revised as needed. At the least, however, it specifies:

- the qualification, units or learning outcomes for which the candidate is seeking credit;
- possible sources of evidence; and
- a date for the submission of the portfolio or a date by which the candidate will be ready for assessment.

Increasingly, education and training providers are seeking agreement from candidates' managers or others in the organisation to ensure that candidates get the internal support they need in order to prepare their action plan. This contract might specify the time or resources that the candidate will have to fulfill the action or assessment plan. Such contracts are serving to help increasing numbers of candidates actually meet their targets.

In some cases, after completing an action assessment plan, candidates need to enrol in a programme before receiving further access to the advisor or group support. In others, candidates need to indicate exactly when and how they plan to collect or generate their evidence *and* progress with new learning. The action or assessment plan is signed and dated by both the advisor and the candidate and each retains a copy.

This final stage of the staged interview is the same for most candidates seeking assessment services through an educational or training provider. The terminology and the time-scale may vary, but all effective flexible assessment services need to develop a comparable action-oriented framework.

Variations on the interview
As with all staged or structured interviews, there are any number of variations possible. In the one just described, for example, there are some employer-based programmes which rely much more on the candidates' self-assessment to encourage reflection and to link their strengths to qualifications and standards or learning outcomes on offer. Working with either workbooks,

checklists or some other form of stimulation, a candidate may not need to meet with his or her advisor except to review and finalise the action or assessment plan.

Similarly, in some employment contexts it is possible for people to work in small groups to develop their profiles and identify their aims, strengths and sources of evidence. In this case the advisor may serve as facilitator to the group, meeting with individual candidates only at the end of the process to sign the action or assessment plan. In still other models, the staged interview may need to take place over several pre-defined sessions.

Materials needed*

As was stated earlier, assessment requires significant monitoring and record-keeping. It is not surprising, therefore, that it often involves a lot of paperwork. A complete and accessible file needs to be maintained for each candidate. Many people – assessors, registrars, quality assurance personnel, the candidates themselves – will need to use the file, so it is important that the documentation is as clear, accurate and up-to-date as possible. What follows is a list and brief description of the forms that might be used to monitor a candidate's progress through the assessment process.

1. *Application form*
All flexible services require candidates to complete some sort of application form which is generally sent to the organisation before the candidate comes for the interview. The application form should be user-friendly with large enough print for the candidates to be able to read the directions and adequate space provided for them to enter their responses. (Many adults complain that the forms used for traditional-aged students are very difficult to read.)

The information requested on the application form will vary

---

* This section has been adapted from OU (1990) *APL: An Open Learning Pack for Advisors and Assessors*.

from one organisation to another. But essentially, it should collect brief information about the candidate's current and past activities and request a statement of why the candidate is seeking credit or recognition.

Some candidates may have difficulty completing the form on their own because of a literacy problem or physical disability. If this is the case, the providing organisation will need to provide the assistance these candidates need. (This is true, of course, for all the other forms and documents candidates may need to complete.)

2. *Checklist of interview stages*
Many advisors find it useful to create a paper or computer-based document by which they can monitor the progress of each candidate during or after the interview itself. They can note the outcomes of each phase and record actions to be taken by the candidate and/or themselves. Such checklists can also provide useful feedback information to the candidates. As other forms and documents are completed and placed in the candidate's file, this checklist can be amended or discarded.

3. *Qualifications on offer in higher education and non-S/NVQ contexts**
Each candidate will need to review a list of the qualifications or programmes on offer for which he or she could seek accreditation of prior learning. In some organisations, such as a college, which has an institutional commitment to offer flexible assessment across all its qualifications and programmes, this presents no major problem. However, some organisations only offer flexible assessment services for a portion of their offerings. Both advisors and candidates need to know what these offerings are.

Even with the best of lists, many candidates will need further explanations about the qualifications or programmes being offered. Although many advisors are used to working with the language (and jargon!), most candidates are not. Advisors

---

* Since April 1996 the use of diverse evidence has become fundamental to all S/NVQ assessments.

should therefore be prepared to answer questions in clear, jargon-free language.

4. Checklists of standards or learning outcomes

All candidates will need to know what is expected of them. They need to be able to equate what they know and can do with what is on offer at the centre. One way for centres to help candidates do this is to develop checklists based on the standards or learning outcomes related to each of the qualifications on offer. Usually it is the assessors or the subject specialists who develop these checklists in consultation with the advisors. Some assessment providers also supply guidelines to candidates on how to complete the checklists and offer examples of completed checklists (with sources of evidence noted) for candidates to review. In conjunction with this, many UK employers are 'translating' the national standard into local language to make sure that they are more readily understood and taken up by their employees.

5. Action or assessment plan

These plans serve as a type of contract between the candidate and the providing organisation. The main purpose of the plan is to:

1. spell out the qualifications or units the candidate is claiming;
2. indicate types of evidence the candidate will be gathering or generating;
3. indicate the time frame in which the portfolio or assessment is to be completed; and
4. provide a space for both the candidate and the advisor to sign and date the agreement or plan.

6. Guide to Personal Report

At the end of the interview, most candidates will begin to generate or gather evidence linked to standards or learning outcomes. An important piece of this evidence is the candidate's own reflective narrative statement, often referred to as a 'personal report'. The purpose of the personal report, which can be written or oral, is to give candidates an opportunity to:

- describe the context in which their learning was achieved;
- highlight particular successes or achievements;
- link outcomes of achievement to the evidence as appropriate;
- reflect knowledge and understanding.

Once completed, these personal reports serve to provide a valuable 'road map' to aid the assessor's understanding of the candidate and the nature of their evidence.

Since the structure and format of personal reports can vary, assessment providers need to provide clear, concise guidelines for learners to help them develop these reports without difficulty.

7.   Guide to portfolio production

Candidates who opt for presenting diverse evidence in a portfolio or some type of file or binder will need guidance too. They need to know the desired structure of the portfolio, the forms needed, and to see examples of acceptable evidence. In general, the better the portfolio guidance, the more likely that candidates will submit stronger, better organised portfolios.

8.   Guide to services

Candidates also need to know what other services are on offer. Are there portfolio development workshops, peer support groups, a video in the library they can refer to or open workshops in which they can develop new skills and knowledge or competence? Flexible assessment organisations should be prepared to develop some sort of guide to services or a candidate resource handbook.

Portfolio production

Following the interview, candidates need to gather or generate their evidence in order to construct their portfolios. During this period, which can last from a matter or weeks to several months, advisors need to be able to provide a range of support. They need to:

- provide information;
- respond to questions;
- review the candidates' work;
- encourage candidates;
- liaise with assessors; and
- give candidates fair and accurate feedback.

They also need to review finished portfolios for completeness, readability and organisation. It is not for the advisor to act as assessor, that is, to determine whether the candidate fully satisfies the specified requirements, but it is the advisor's job to help the candidate present him or herself in the best possible light. Advisors must guard against doing the candidate's job. One of the strengths of the process is that the onus of responsibility is on the candidate. Advisors are there to offer a helping hand; but it is the candidate who must do the work.

Adult development issues

Knowing about and understanding adult development issues can help advisors, assessors and work-place mentors to support candidates more effectively through the assessment process. Adults are often more focused and more aware of their own goals, but at the same time lack confidence to take action. They may be balancing all the adult roles of partner, parent, worker, and community volunteer and feel they have very little time left for themselves. Flexible assessment, with its emphasis on self-direction is often a way by which adults can find a bit of time to focus on their own needs. It is therefore essential that they make the best use of the time available to them to progress through the assessment process. As we have already noted, they will look to the providing institution to provide support, minimise red tape, and actively help them reach their goals.

Many professionals new to competence-based assessment systems find it useful to read some of the background literature about adult development and adult-learning issues. They find that it helps them to understand not only more about the people they find themselves working with but also about themselves, as professionals and as adult learners.

There is a growing body of excellent literature emerging in this field and no doubt most college and university libraries will provide ample reading material for the interested reader. However, a few of the more pioneering thinkers may provide a useful starting point for additional investigation; a list is given at the end of this chapter.

Summary

The role of the advisor in flexible assessment is primarily one of supporting and mentoring candidates through the process. To do this effectively, it is necessary for the advisor or work-based mentor to demonstrate a range of skills. They need to be able to work *with* candidates rather than *for* candidates in helping them reflect on their skills and accomplishments.

The advisor has to be prepared to work with a wide range of candidates. Candidates will vary considerably in terms of their skills and accomplishments as well as in terms of their motivation and commitment to the learning and assessment programme. The advisor must be flexible enough to work with all candidates in the most appropriate manner: empowering and stimulating interest in those who lack self confidence, whilst providing facts and figures for others.

Advisors also need to be able to offer specific guidance and advice for candidates when they are generating and gathering evidence. However, throughout the process, it is the candidates themselves who must assume responsibility for the evidence and its presentation, not their advisors. Advisors need to be good listeners to respond fully to candidates' varied needs in the most sensitive and effective way possible.

Further reading

Covey, S R (1992) *The Seven Habits of Highly Effective People*, Simon & Schuster Ltd, London.

Cross, K P (1981) *Adults as Learners: Increasing Participation and Facilitating Learning*, Jossey-Bass, San Francisco.

Cross, K P (1986) *Adults as Learners*, Jossey-Bass, San Francisco.

Gould, R (1978) *Transformations: Growth and Change in Adult Life*, Simon & Schuster, New York.

Knowles, M S (1970) *The Modern Practice of Adult Education: Andragogy Versus Pedagogy*, Association Press, New York.

Kolb, D A (1976) *Learning Styles Inventory: Technical Manual*, McBer and Company, Boston.

Levinson, D, Darrow, C N, Klein, E G, Levinson, M H and McKee, B (1978) *The Seasons of a Man's Life*, Knopf, New York.

Parsloe, E (1992) *Coaching, Mentoring and Assessing: A Practical Guide to Developing Competence*, Kogan Page Ltd, London.

Chapter 4

Providing for Groups

Introduction

Although advisors can and do provide significant support to candidates individually, increasingly institutions offering flexible assessment services are introducing group activities to assist candidates. The reasons for this are many. First, many organisations, including employers, have found that providing the one-to-one support described in the last chapter can be expensive. They have come to realise that providing services to groups of candidates can significantly reduce the time required of any particular advisor or mentor. They also have found that although some candidates most assuredly require considerable support individually, some do not, and that those who can are quite satisfied to work with less extensive one-to-one support.

Second, some candidates actually prefer *not* to work individually with an advisor; they prefer the familiarity of working with other adults like themselves who are aiming for a common goal. They are happy to progress at their own pace with a variety of written materials, peer support and an occasional conversation with the advisor. Working in groups can also promote team building, help individuals interpret the standards or learning outcomes, and increase motivation. This has been found to be particularly true in employment contexts.

Third, many professionals who provide flexible assessment advice and support have expressed concern that adults choosing to acquire qualifications through more learner-centred approaches rather than through traditional means may lose out on vital learning interactions that often occur during traditional educational and training instruction. They believe that when people work together there is an important learning experience that occurs which enhances the development of each individual. Advisors have also reported that candidates working in groups often avoid the feelings of isolation sometimes expressed by those candidates who do not have group support options.

For all of these reasons, and no doubt others, colleges, universities, employers and others who offer flexible assessment services are developing a variety of ways to work with groups. This chapter will review in detail some of the options open to professionals wishing to develop a number of group activities as part of their service.

Assessment orientation sessions

One of the most popular ways of introducing potential candidates to the competence-based assessment process is through orientation sessions. Whether one hour or three, these sessions often serve to introduce potential candidates to the assessment process for the first time. They allow potential candidates to meet others like themselves and to ask questions about the assessment process and the likely outcomes. Many orientation sessions also encourage potential candidates to begin to reflect on (self-assess) what they know and can do. This is a critical first step in the assessment process.

These sessions are useful to help individuals to learn about the qualifications on offer and, in the context of S/NVQs, to become familiar with the unit structure of these awards. Experience in employment settings highlights the importance of the senior management fully participating in these orientation sessions. Their participation provides a valuable and highly visible way to communicate the organisation's commitment to the process and the desired outcome of helping individuals assume greater responsibility for their own development and assessment.

The orientation session occurs at the pre-entry stage. Its primary purpose is to increase potential candidates' awareness of the assessment process, describe its value and generally help individuals decide whether or not they wish to embark on the APL route.

An effective orientation session must provide information, facilitate communication and enable individuals to have their questions answered. It should be well organised and delivered in an interesting, friendly manner.

Usually advisors or mentors deliver these sessions and most often they use a variety of techniques to illustrate their points, disseminate information, facilitate discussion, and encourage feedback and questions from the participants. To no small extent it is the advisor's presentation and listening skills that will determine the effectiveness of the session.

Orientation session participants

Before an advisor or mentor can effectively plan for the orientation session, he or she must be clear about who the participants will be. The advisor responsible for the session will want to know well in advance who is likely to attend and what their primary purposes are in seeking recognition for their skills and knowledge.

Often in education or training contexts, orientation sessions are open to any interested adult. Others may be designed for homogeneous groups, for example, managers from a particular company or other occupationally-specific groups. Still others may be organised around the needs of a particular community group. Although the basic information the advisor will want to convey is the same, the tone, examples, and responses to particular questions may differ considerably.

The level of literacy skills of the potential candidates may be another important factor which influences the content and manner of the briefing session. Clearly if the potential candidates have limited reading ability, advisors will need to rely more on oral communication than written. They also may find that people with reading problems lack self-confidence in other areas of their lives. The advisor may therefore need to plan different types of activities or group discussions to encourage the development of people's self-confidence.

Similarly, there may be people within any potential candidate group who have special needs. Every effort should be made to provide for these individuals too, whether that means ensuring that the venue can be accessed by wheelchair, that large-print versions of some materials are available, or that oral communication takes precedence over the use of writen material. Often very small modifications in a given programme or venue can make all the difference to people with special needs. If a potential client group speaks English as a second language, some materials might also be offered in the participants' own language.

The orientation session venue

Potential candidates may come to the orientation session quite nervous. Every effort should be made to welcome them and make sure they are comfortable. The session should be held in a well-lit, well-ventilated room that is easily accessible and clean. There should be adequate public transport or parking with clear directions provided to candidates well in advance of the session.

Most orientation session rooms should be large enough to accommodate the full group – perhaps up to 25 people – but be small enough so that people can be encouraged to speak in small groups. If possible, tables with five or six chairs often work well for the group discussions. Toilets should be near the room and of course ramps or other facilities provided for people with disabilities.

Time of day and length of session

Orientation sessions should be held on days and at times convenient to the participants. If the participants are employed,

75

for example, the session might be held in the evening or on Saturday. If the session is intended for people who are primarily unemployed, the session might be conveniently organised during the day. Alternatively, if the session is to be held on the premises of a particular employer, then the employer will in all likelihood identify the best time of day to hold the session. There is no single best time to hold an orientation session: the best time is one that is convenient to the participants and the convener.

The length of an orientation session will depend on a number of factors, not the least of which are the expected outcomes of the session. Most sessions are held for two to four hours. Longer sessions are sometimes organised, but these usually include additional purposes, eg they provide ample opportunity for self-assessment for individuals' personal career development.

Most advisors and mentors find that with experience they are flexible enough to offer orientation sessions of varying lengths, depending on the needs of the groups, the context in which the session is being offered and any other factors unique to the particular situation.

Refreshments

As with other training or educational events, the availability of light refreshments – tea, coffee, or fruit juice – often contributes to a more welcoming, friendly atmosphere. Many participants may not have attended an educational or training event for many years; offering them light refreshment is one way to help them relax. People coming from work or other commitments may be especially appreciative. Clearly, though, however desirable it may be to have refreshments available, this is a matter that can only be determined by the local situation and available resources.

Materials and audio-visual aids

At the orientation session, advisors will want to have all the relevant materials they need to conduct the session. Materials might include brochures or leaflets about S/NVQs or other qualifications, the range of support services available, a listing of fees, a schedule or portfolio of development workshops (as appropriate), the learning or training options offered, an application form, etc.

The materials themselves should be informative, readable and easy to use. If possible, participants should have information to take home with them so they can reflect on the options and discuss them with family or friends. The orientation session facilitator will have to make sure that all of the materials have a clear purpose and are relevant to the needs of the group. It is important to guard against overwhelming participants with too much paper or information. An abundance of 'required' reading can discourage people from moving ahead.

As with any effective public presentation, the use of interesting audio-visual materials can serve to enhance the communication and understanding between the facilitator and the group. Key points about the assessment and development opportunities and the assessment process itself can be well illustrated on slides, overhead transparencies, video, or through multi-media presentations.

Clearly each facilitator needs to use materials and techniques with which he or she feels comfortable. But as has been emphasised elsewhere in this book, different people have different ways of learning things and may respond more or less positively to any one. For that reason, it is often a good idea for advisors to develop more than one way to convey the messages delivered during the orientation session.

A team approach

Most advisors learn to conduct different types of orientation sessions. Depending on the context in which they are working, the number of people expected at the session, the resources available and other factors, some centres take a team approach in delivering orientation sessions.

Sometimes two advisors work together or an assessor contributes to an advisor's presentation. In some centres successful candidates are invited to provide a brief input and respond to participants' questions. In others, workplace managers or an Industrial Training Organisation (ITO) representative may contribute. Many other options are possible, of course. It is up to each centre to determine the most appropriate people to deliver the orientation session.

If more than one person is delivering separate sessions, however, it is important for the centre to make sure that staff are doing so in comparable ways and do not contradict each other. If the content, time frame, activities and materials are developed by the team of people who are to deliver the session, there is greater likelihood that participants will have similar, if not identical, orientation session experiences. Regular reviews and evaluations of the sessions should be undertaken, and systematic evaluation feedback collected from all participants.

Content of the orientation session

The exact content of a briefing session will vary from one context to another and depend on a number of other factors already cited. However, almost all follow a similar basic framework that includes:

- welcome and introductions;
- the purpose of the session;
- an overview of the purpose and process of flexible assessment;
- the likely benefit of the process and the outcomes;
- an introduction to the standards, learning outcomes, courses or programmes on offer;
- an introduction to the nature of evidence;
- a question and answer period; and
- a closing session.

Most orientation sessions include some sort of ice-breaker at the beginning of the programme and an opportunity for each member of the group to tell something about him or herself. This not only allows the advisor to learn something about each group member, it also begins to foster the early stages of reflection for each participant.

The overview of the assessment process should describe the main benefits to the participants, the steps needed to be taken, and the roles of the key people. It should also describe the separate responsibilities of the advisor or mentor, assessor and the candidate during each of the stages and provide a clear idea of the range of support services offered by the centre.

To understand fully the process and the likely benefits, each participant will need an opportunity to consider the standards, learning outcomes and/or qualifications on offer. As part of the initial self-reflection process, participants might be invited to complete mini check-lists of competences they might be claiming, or discuss in structured small group discussions their accomplishments or areas of strength.

The concept of evidence is best introduced by giving participants an opportunity to see one or more examples of portfolios and/or generating their own lists of evidence in a structured group activity led by the advisor. This has been rated as *essential* by successful candidates who have initially asked, 'How can you be expected to develop a portfolio unless you know what you are aiming for?' Even at this early stage, advisors should help the participants understand the breadth of acceptable evidence and some of the criteria by which assessors will judge it.

Throughout the session, the facilitator(s) should encourage the prospective candidates to ask questions and identify areas of concern. The facilitator will also want to provide a clear picture of the various steps people can take as a result of attending the session:

1. Begin the development and assessment process;
2. Embark on another learning option;
3. Consider the options, and make a decision later on.

The closing session should thank people for coming and provide an opportunity for the potential candidates to ask any further questions.

Portfolio development workshops

The portfolio development workshop is another effective way of working with candidates in groups. Unlike the orientation session, which is for *potential* candidates, the portfolio development workshop is intended to support people already committed to the assessment process. These workshops are generally offered during stage three of the process, gathering and generating evidence.

There are several basic purposes served by portfolio development workshops. These include:

- motivating the candidate to reflect or analyse his/her past accomplishments and current competence;
- discussing and interpreting the standards or learning outcomes;
- helping the candidate to select or develop the most appropriate evidence for his/her portfolio;
- helping the candidate construct his/her portfolio; and
- preparing the candidate for assessment.

Research has shown that candidates who make use of the portfolio development workshop and go on to complete the process, do so with increased self-confidence, heightened self-awareness, and a greater ability to organise and integrate information (Warren and Breen, 1976; Hall, 1991).

The design

Portfolio development workshops can be designed in many different ways and can be offered for different periods of time.

Some centres run portfolio development workshops on an open basis so that candidates can drop in and out over several months, depending on their needs. This is especially effective in workplace contexts, particularly at lunch time or immediately after work. For these sessions, a single facilitator or advisor is present to respond to questions, organise small group discussions and otherwise serve as a resource to the candidates who show up.

Other centres provide a more structured approach, with each of several sessions focusing on particular points or issues. Generally, these sessions are also facilitated by a single advisor, although sometimes assessors are invited to discuss with the group particular issues relating to the meaning of the standards and the acceptability of the evidence.

Still other centres, most often colleges and universities, offer portfolio development courses for credit in and of themselves, regardless of the outcomes of the assessment of the candidates' portfolios. In these cases the course is usually organised around a particular theme such as the development of academic or vocational skills, personal or career development, the meaning of education, careers orientation, etc (Michelson and Mandell, 1988). In this model, candidates produce their portfolios as an outcome of the course.

Lastly, some centres offer periodic portfolio development workshops, often only three to four hours in length. This single session is designed to cover two basic topics: acceptable evidence and the construction of the portfolio. These sessions are usually intended to supplement other written materials and are offered primarily to motivate and provide candidates with more concrete hands-on information about portfolio development.

Many of the points made about orientation sessions are applicable, of course, to portfolio development workshops as well: the need for an appropriate venue, the desirability of refreshments, the use of clear and relevant materials and audio-visual aids, etc. What follows is a detailed description of the essential content of portfolio development workshops which will be applicable to most candidates' needs, regardless of the type of workshop offered or its duration. Variations can be developed based on the additional needs of the candidates, the requirements of the providing organisations or options developed by the advisors offering the workshops.

It is important to add that the content of the portfolio development workshop can also be used to advise and support candidates in one-on-one situations or on-line.

The content

The content of portfolio development workshops generally falls into four categories:

1. understanding the standards;
2. defining the nature of acceptable evidence;
3. constructing the portfolio; and
4. preparing for assessment.

We will look at each of these in detail.

Understanding the standards

Portfolio development workshops provide an excellent forum in which candidates can come to understand and use the standards. Candidates are better able to develop their evidence and prepare for assessment when they understand the standards or learning outcomes on offer, and see the relevance to their own local situation.

Using the standards in the portfolio development workshop also allows candidates to continue the reflection and iterative process of flexible assessment. By working with the standards, reflecting on their own understanding of them, candidates often come to see their achievements in a new light. Things they may have forgotten are remembered; experiences that once seemed random suddenly fall into place as part of a previously unperceived learning pattern.

Advisors, working with assessors, in advance of the portfolio development workshops, need to make sure that candidates have access to all the information necessary to use and understand the standards. As stressed earlier, examples of previously prepared portfolios or particular experiences of other candidates can be particularly helpful.

Diverse evidence

The concept of diverse evidence stems from the very notion of assessment itself. In the context of the emerging S/NVQs described in the first chapter (and the Appendix), assessment is defined as:

> The gathering and interpretation of evidence based on the candidates' performance as judged against the standards (elements of competence and performance criteria). The purpose of assessment is to confirm when candidates are competent and entitled to accreditation.

All assessment requires evidence. It is important for advisors and candidates alike to understand the basic concept of evidence. Whether we make an informal assessment, eg, 'It's raining, therefore I need my umbrella', or a more formal one, eg, 'This job applicant seems to meet my requirements and has presented very strong letters of recommendation', we are using evidence to make assessment judgements.

In the first example, we have *observed* the rain (gathered direct evidence) and this has helped us to make the decision to carry an umbrella. In the second example, we have probably interviewed the candidate (gathered direct evidence) and have reviewed letters about the candidate (gathered indirect evidence) before making the decision about whether or not to hire the applicant. Throughout our lives we use evidence in this way, no matter how small or large or how formal or informal our decision-making process.

One of the first principles, then, in introducing candidates to the idea of diverse evidence is to convey that they have been collecting evidence and making decisions based on that evidence since they were babies. The concept of evidence should not be new to anyone. It should be seen as a natural, everyday phenomenon.

It is also useful to help candidates think of the many ways they previously have been assessed either during their formal education or in employment: they may have been observed, produced reports, completed special projects, taken written examinations, participated in classroom discussions – all of these activities are methods by which teachers and supervisors routinely gather evidence to make grading, ranking or pay award decisions.

Once candidates have a clear idea about the general nature of diverse evidence, it is important to help them think about the specific forms of evidence they will need to generate or gather as they work towards a unit or qualification. They need to recognise that the nature of their evidence will be largely in their control. Just as no two candidates will have identical experiences, so no two candidates will present exactly the same evidence.

Candidates need to know that assessors will be expecting to see diverse forms of evidence generated by the candidate him- or herself and often by someone else too. Any given candidate will generally be expected to generate three types of evidence:

- a personal report or narrative statement, produced by the candidate orally or in writing;
- evidence of performance, again produced by the candidate;
- indirect evidence *about* the candidate, produced by someone else.

The personal report gives the assessor a 'road map' to the candidate's skills and knowledge and the context in which the candidate has demonstrated his or her competence or learning achievements. It also provides an opportunity for the candidate to reflect on and describe his or her successes and to provide insight into the process that led to the desired outcome and the nature of the supporting evidence.

The evidence of performance can be generated through direct observation of performance by the supervisor or assessor. For example, as part of his or her normal duties, a supervisor may observe the candidate on several different occasions carrying out his or her normal duties. Based on these observations, the supervisor will determine whether or not the candidate has met the standards. Sometimes, of course, direct observation of performance is not always possible, in which case candidates may be asked to participate in a simulation or role play exercise. Once again the supervisor or assessor would use the actual performance to make his or her assessment decisions.

Alternatively, sometimes direct observation is neither possible nor cost effective, in which case the products or outcomes of performance can be used. Examples of such products include:

- computer programmes;
- financial reports;
- lesson plans;
- musical compositions;
- training manuals;
- components;
- operations schedules etc.

These examples – including the actual observed performance evidence – are often called **direct evidence**. All stem directly from the candidate's own efforts, whether in waged or unwaged situations.

However, sometimes it is not possible for candidates to produce direct evidence related to all of the standards or learning outcomes under assessment. In these instances, candidates will want to bring forward examples of **indirect evidence**. These examples of diverse evidence tell the assessor *about* the candidate. Examples may include:

- letters of validation from past or current employers;
- special awards or certificates;
- newspaper articles about the candidate;
- photographs of the candidate's work etc.

Generally, direct evidence is considered stronger than indirect evidence. Increasingly, however, assessors are finding that the 'triangulation' of evidence works best in many contexts: that is, the candidate's own statement; direct performance evidence (either through observation or through products); and one or more statements about the candidate from others. Like a three legged stool, this model of diverse evidence holds up well. Of course, both the candidate and the assessor will need to pay careful consideration to any specific evidence requirements within the standards or qualifications towards which they are working.

Portfolio development workshops need to provide ample opportunity for candidates to identify and explore these various forms of diverse evidence. The following case studies may help to illustrate the point.

Case Study

One manager seeking recognition of her competence to monitor and control the use of resources presented the following evidence as part of a portfolio of evidence:

1. a personal report that described the problem she faced, the alternatives available to her and her organisation, her decision-making process, and a verbal summary of the outcomes of her work;
2. a proposal she had prepared that related to the improvement she had recommended;
3. memos written by her and others detailing the outcomes of several meetings she had had with her line manager and external suppliers detailing the proposed changes;
4. annual financial reports, showing the cost savings that resulted from the implementation of her proposal;
5. after the assessor had reviewed this and other evidence, the manager also responded to a series of oral questions about her work and role, posed by the assessor.

In this example, the candidate was able to generate direct evidence (1,

2, some of 3, 4 and 5) and indirect evidence (in the form of memos written by others about the candidate's actions and decisions).

Case Study

Another candidate seeking accreditation for several NVQ units in customer service was observed by his supervisor (the assessor) on agreed occasions over a period of six months. After each formal observation, the supervisor discussed the candidate's performance in terms of the standards, asked questions and gave feedback. The candidate also kept a log of his interactions with a range of clients during this period, noting the particular problems he had to address and how he brought the various situations to resolution. In addition, he maintained a small file of letters he had received during the period from clients thanking him for his efforts.

In this example, the candidate generated two forms of direct evidence in the form of the supervisor's observations and his own log of interactions with clients. He supplemented these with the indirect evidence he received in the form of letters from the clients.

As these examples illustrate, candidates need to think about generating or collecting the strongest evidence they can. The portfolio development workshop may be the best place to begin this process of reflecting and identifying a range of appropriate diverse evidence.

The workshop also needs to help candidates understand what the assessor(s) will be looking for as part of the assessment process, in particular authenticity and currency.

1. *Authenticity*: Assessors will want to ensure that the work submitted by the candidate really is the result of his or her own effort. There are many ways that candidates can provide evidence of the authenticity of their work, particularly if they are submitting evidence of prior achievements. They can present letters from others to substantiate their evidence; they can submit additional corroborative evidence; they can prepare a

substantiated narrative statement; or they can be prepared to answer questions posed by the assessor about the evidence.

Sometimes if candidates have been part of a team effort, the issue of authenticity presents unique problems for both the candidate and the assessor. In this case, candidates usually must provide one or more additional pieces of evidence which clearly attest to the candidate's own accomplishments or contributions to the group's work.

2. *Currency:* The concept of currency relates to how recent the evidence is. In most cases candidates will need to be given clear guidelines regarding this matter. For example, in the area of information technology, evidence more than one or two years old might be deemed too old and therefore inappropriate. On the other hand, a writer or journalist may well be able to submit evidence one or two years old, assuming it was relevant to the standards or learning outcomes in place.

During the portfolio development workshops, candidates need to be given the opportunity to work with the concepts of authenticity and currency to make sure they can accurately apply them to the preparation of their own portfolios of diverse evidence.

Selecting evidence
To help individuals select their evidence, the advisor or mentor needs to assist candidates during the portfolio development workshop to focus on the *outcomes* of their learning. There is a great tendency among adults to want to provide information about the *process* of learning something. If clear standards or learning outcomes are in place, however, the emphasis must be on the products of the candidate's achievements. This is not always an easy task, particularly since the outcomes of a candidate's performance may not yield concrete evidence.

For example, consider a probation officer who lacks a formal qualification but who has been performing his job competently for a number of years. One of his main responsibilities may be to support offenders during the period of probation. The officer may meet with a particular offender on a regular basis, provide information, guidance and advice and still the offender may break his or her probation restrictions. Does this mean that the probation officer has not done a good job and would not have evidence of his competence as a probation officer if he were to seek flexible assessment services to gain a formal qualification?

In this example, as with many other helping or service occupations, it is indeed a range of processes for which the candidate must show evidence. Hopefully, these processes would be spelled out clearly in the standards. For example, responsibilities of a probation officer might be to:
Assist clients to make use of available services and information.
(Care Sector Consortium, 1990)

To do this, the standards might further specify that the probation officer should be able to:
Assist the client to access services and facilities, and
Encourage the client to use services and facilities.

The candidate would therefore be expected to provide evidence that he had assisted and encouraged the client to access and use various services and facilities. There are many ways that this evidence could be provided, through written reports, memos, authenticated interviews, perhaps even a video or audio tape. The fact that the offender broke parole, although an unfortunate outcome, may not be attributable to the probation officer's lack of competence.

So although the focus is on the outcomes of achievements, candidates need to:

1. be directed by the standards;
2. see that some of the outcomes of their efforts in work or other activities may not provide the most useful or appropriate type of evidence needed;
3. whenever possible, seek assessment options that include observation and discussion of their performance.

Many academic and vocational areas lend themselves to product evidence: art, design, composing, computer programing, management, engineering, horticulture – all of these and many other occupational or academic areas are based on product evidence. Candidates coming from these areas seeking recognition for their prior learning generally have little difficulty in identifying products to help them prove their competence.

Sometimes candidates seek recognition or credit in areas for which they have little or no evidence. For example, a local history buff or someone interested in philosophy may not be able to generate any substantial proof of their learning. In cases such as these, it is up to the advisor to help candidates prepare for other types of assessment – special projects, oral questioning, etc – which are discussed in the next chapter.

In selecting their evidence, candidates also need to think about its relevance. They need to make sure that what they are presenting is directly related to the standards for which they are trying to prove competence. They also need to be reminded that assessors are more interested in the *quality* of the evidence than in the quantity. An abundance of evidence may actually undermine a candidate's claim if it is not relevant to the learning outcomes or standards on offer or is not of sufficient breadth or diversity.

Letters of validation
Special mention must be made about letters of validation. These are useful sources of indirect evidence that many candidates include in their portfolios. During portfolio development workshops, candidates need to receive information on how to request these letters and how to make sure they obtain the type of information they need from the letter writer.

First and foremost it is essential that candidates remember that it is their own responsibility to obtain the letters of validation they need, not the centre's or the advisor's. Candidates must carefully consider who they might approach to request a letter of validation. It need not be a current supervisor. Many candidates request letters of validation from previous supervisors, clients or colleagues. They may also request them of people who know of their work outside the work environment. For example, people in the voluntary sector may be able to obtain a letter from a regional director, or from the accountant, bank manager, public relations officer – anyone who is familiar with the candidate's work and is willing to write on his or her behalf.

To request a letter of validation, candidates will need to:

1. specify the purpose of the letter and the date by which the candidate needs the letter;
2. spell out the competences or learning outcomes for which he or she is seeking recognition or accreditation (explicit standards are very helpful here);
3. provide the name and address of the person to whom the letter should be sent; and
4. as a courtesy include a stamped, properly addressed envelope.

The candidate should also plan to thank the letter writer in advance and provide information on how he or she can be reached should the letter writer have questions.

Most letters of validation are sent to the advisor, who then passes them on to the candidate for inclusion in the portfolio. However, some letter writers prefer to send the letters directly to candidates.

Many centres provide a prototype of a letter to help candidates develop their own letters of validation and in some cases centres also provide written guidelines for the letter writers themselves. An example of such a letter, which has been adapted from material produced by the Open University (OU, 1990) is shown in Figure 4.1.

During the portfolio development workshop, candidates should be given an opportunity to develop their letters of validation and/or request clarification about their preparation from the advisor.

Constructing the portfolio

The portfolio development workshop also needs to provide candidates with clear instructions and guidance on the construction of their portfolios. The better organised a portfolio is, the

Dear _____ ,

Thank you for agreeing to write a letter of validation on behalf of an assessment candidate from this centre. As you are no doubt aware, this assessment process enables individuals to receive recognition and accreditation for skills they have learned in a variety of ways. Your letter will help the centre determine whether or not the candidate has attained the competences he or she has claimed. While your letter may play a critical role in the candidate's assessment, it may not be used as the sole source of information. Most candidates are assessed in a variety of ways.

To be most helpful, your letter should be typed on company or business notepaper and contain the following:

- the candidate's name;
- the date(s) of his or her employment or association with you;
- the post(s) held by the candidate or a description of the capacity in which you know/knew him or her;
- a list of the competences the candidate is claiming and to which you are attesting; and
- your signature and position.

Thank your for your time and assistance in preparing this letter.

Figure 4.1 *A sample candidate letter*

easier it is to assess. For this reason, flexible assessment centres are encouraged to provide specific guidelines on the construction of portfolios.

While any number of options are possible, experience suggests that the most effective portfolios contain the following sections:

1. A cover which contains the name, address and day-time phone number of the candidate. The purpose of the cover is to identify the candidate at a glance and to provide easy access to his or her contact telephone number.

2. A table of contents listing each section and its starting page number. As in all written material, a table of contents offers the reader a clear map to the contents of the document.

3. A narrative statement, personal report, completed checklist or detailed CV which relates the candidate's competences to the standards, units or learning outcomes being claimed. The purpose of this section is to show a clear relationship between what the candidate did and what he or she is claiming. Many assessors find that when they review the evidence in a portfolio, they have difficulty understanding the context in which the evidence was produced. Increasingly, therefore, candidates are being asked to provide sufficient detail about their background, the competences they are claiming and the evidence they are submitting to help the assessors understand exactly what they have accomplished as represented by the evidence in the portfolio.

4. A cross-reference system relating the evidence to the units, elements of competence or learning outcomes being claimed. Again, candidates need to provide clear guidance in their portfolios so that the assessors can easily consider the evidence in relation to the particular units or learning outcomes being claimed. Since some pieces of evidence may support the claim for more than one unit or learning outcome, candidates need to show the assessor exactly what their intention is for each piece of evidence.

5. The evidence itself. Each piece of evidence needs to be clearly labelled to avoid confusion and to make sure the assessor can easily identify the reason it has been included in the portfolio.

During the portfolio development workshop, candidates will

need to review each of these sections, receive whatever guidance the centre normally provides, and have a chance to ask questions about each section. In many portfolio development workshops, candidates are given an opportunity to develop their narrative statements and receive feedback from their peers and/or the advisor.

Preparation of the portfolio

'Neatness counts' is an old adage that still holds true. In preparing their portfolios candidates need to be reminded to use standard English, to make sure they amend spelling and grammatical errors and that they organise their work clearly and effectively. Although most assessors will not be assessing the language or organisation *per se*, the readability of the portfolio is important. If assessors find themselves struggling to understand what a candidate has included in his or her portfolio, they will often be dismissive of the evidence itself. The message from assessors is clear: candidates should take care to present their portfolios as neatly and clearly as possible.

Preparing for assessment

Portfolio development workshops must also help candidates to prepare for assessment more generally. Candidates should have a clear idea of what will happen to their portfolios once they are complete and know what the assessor will be looking for during his or her review of the evidence. Advisors must be prepared to respond to a wide range of questions on this topic since most candidates, with good reason, want to know what will happen to their work.

As time allows, advisors will want to introduce candidates to the various methods of assessment as described in the next chapter and provide role play or simulation opportunities for the candidates to develop an idea of what each method of assessment is like. It cannot be over-stated that many adults hold deep-seated fears of being tested or assessed. Often they have a keen sense of anxiety or even failure from their earlier days as students. The portfolio development workshop should encourage candidates to see that they have significant control of the assessment process and that they have an opportunity to work *with* the assessor, not just respond *to* his or her requests.

Portfolio development workshops also offer candidates an opportunity to see the purpose behind assessment. So often in traditional assessment situations, the person being assessed sees little reason beyond a grade or score for being evaluated. It is hoped that during the portfolio development workshop, candidates will come to see the reasons for the assessment and link these to their own learning and development goals.

Approaches to portfolio development workshops

Portfolio development workshops can provide an exciting opportunity for adults to develop not just their portfolios but themselves. The workshops can offer a focus for reflection unknown to most of us. They can also provide a structured environment in which the candidates have time to consider their achievements and organise their evidence. Although many people can work on their own, the portfolio development workshop provides a valuable opportunity for both the candidates and their advisors.

Most portfolio development workshops include a great deal of small group work. A certain amount of guidance and input is required of the advisor or facilitator, but the real learning opportunities often take place in small group discussions or when candidates receive feedback from one or more members of the workshop or when common problems are tackled by the group.

Organisers of the portfolio development workshops need to make sure that there is ample time for candidates to draw on the resources of the group and to voice their own opinions and issues. In some programmes, portfolio development workshops are combined with peer-support groups. These groups meet on an informal basis to help one another in the development of their portfolios. Since no advisor or facilitator is required, these groups can be an efficient and cost-effective way of encouraging candidates to help themselves.

Summary

Group activities are increasingly being used by education and training providers and employers to support candidates through the assessment process. Staff at these organisations recognise that group activities can be more cost-effective than one-to-one advice and that they provide a useful framework for many adults. Experience at a wide range of centres indicates that candidates themselves often prefer working with peers to share their mutual experiences and address common problems. Advisors also recognise that group work helps reduce some candidates' feelings of isolation, stimulates valuable interactions and motivates candidates to achieve their goals.

There are a number of group-based activities professionals use to deliver flexible assessment services. The initial orientation session is one which allows people to learn about the process and ask questions before they decide whether or not to proceed.

Portfolio development workshops provide another opportunity to work with groups. Candidates can analyse their experiences, identify appropriate evidence, develop their portfolios and prepare for assessment. In portfolio development workshops an advisor can explain to a group of candidates essential information about selecting, gathering and generating evidence, preparing letters of validation, constructing portfolios, preparing for assessment and so forth. To do this on an individual basis would obviously require more time and does not allow for valuable sharing of experiences by the participating candidates.

Chapter 5

Assessment and Quality Assurance

Assessment takes place during the fourth stage of the learner-centred assessment process. It is the critical activity on which the entire system rests. To no small degree, the credibility of the outcome depends almost exclusively on the validity, reliability and fairness of the assessment process. For this reason, it is essential that those planning to establish a sound flexible assessment service learn about and adhere to principles of good practice in assessment. Many of these principles are reflected in the assessor units of the TDLB standards, which are referred to throughout this chapter.

Just what are these principles of good practice? For our purposes, they include a range of technical requirements *and* a range of effective communication skills. In this chapter we look at both.

To begin, flexible assessment does not require highly specialised training or skills in test design and statistics. Rather, flexible assessment requires assessors who are familiar with and up-to-date in their fields and the standards that relate to the occupation or area of study to be assessed, and are reasonably effective communicators (Docking, 1990a). These assessments, like all others, require the assessor to draw inferences about the candidate's performance based on the evidence generated and presented by the candidate. It requires the assessor to go through a systematic process that will satisfy the candidate, the advisor, other assessors and internal and external verifiers that the

97

assessment and the resulting decisions were made as validly, reliably and fairly as possible.

Teachers and trainers regularly administer tests and other assessment instruments. These include paper and pencil examinations developed by the teacher; norm-referenced examinations developed and scored by a central body or organisation; special projects; performance-based skills tests; classroom participation; or even attendance. In these instances it is the professional test maker, the teacher or trainer who determines the nature of the assessment and the nature of the evidence to be used – what form it takes, the content it will cover, when it will be administered, how it will be scored or graded.

Most of these assessments are also directly related to the subject matter being *taught*. The teacher or trainer 'teaches' certain materials and assumes that the students or trainees learn them. The assessment, therefore, serves as a check that the students have acquired the skills and knowledge facilitated by the teacher. In these traditional situations, the teacher or trainer maintains almost complete control over the assessment and the nature of the evidence used to draw the necessary inferences during the assessment process.

During competence-based assessments, however, the assessor *shares* control of the assessment process with the candidate. Although it is the assessor who makes the final decision regarding the outcome of the assessment, the candidate has considerable leeway in developing and presenting the evidence to be used in the assessment. Since these assessments are not linked to any *particular* training or learning programme, it is assumed that a variety of diverse evidence can be used during the assessment process. Assessors, subject specialists knowledgeable about the standards or learning outcomes, must come to anticipate and value the diversity of evidence that can be used by candidates to meet these. Although assessors do not and cannot control the exact nature of the evidence candidates submit, they still must ensure that the evidence meets the technical requirements of any sound assessment.

Technical requirements

There are essentially five technical requirements that all assessments must meet. These include:

- validity
- reliability
- sufficiency
- authenticity
- currency.

Validity

Validity refers to how well the assessment matches what is being assessed. Consider, for example, the UK driving test. During the assessment the candidate is asked to drive the car under natural road conditions. While the candidate drives, the assessor notes how the individual handles the car, responds to road conditions and/or any emergencies that might crop up, performs particular manoeuvres and in general meets the specified standards of safe driving. A written test would not be considered a valid test of an individual's ability to drive a car.

Extending the example a bit further, however, some people argue that the driving test is not as valid as it should be since it does not test the driver's ability to drive on the motorways or at night. In this instance the examiner (assessor) gathers no direct information about the candidate's ability to drive in these situations. At the end of the road test, however, the examiner asks the driver a set of questions, some of which pertain to driving at night and on the motorway. These oral questions serve to test the candidate's knowledge and understanding, from which the assessor draws further inferences about the candidate's ability. A candidate suffering from night blindness, though, might be able to answer the questions correctly but still be unable to drive safely in darkness. The oral examination then, while not in and of itself a valid assessment of a person's ability to drive, serves to extend the valid evidence collected during the actual road test, allowing the examiner to draw further inferences. For a number of reasons, not the least of which is cost, the day-time driving test is seen as sufficiently valid to allow a person who passes to drive under all circumstances.*

Another way of thinking about validity is to consider the notion of relevance. Is the evidence relevant or indicative of what is being assessed? Does the evidence match what is being looked for? Making sure the evidence is relevant – valid – is one way of contributing to 'getting the assessment right'. In many assessments – whether about people or things – there is an attempt to minimise the margin of error in the inferences being drawn. Using valid evidence is one of the most critical paths towards this desired goal.

Reliability

Reliability refers to the consistency of the assessment outcome. An assessment is considered reliable to the extent that different assessors using the same evidence make comparable judgements; or that the same assessor over time makes similar judgements. In competence-based assessment it is assumed that different candidates will present different evidence. Thus in the current context, reliability is about assessors placing similar value on pieces of evidence and making similar judgements when confronted with the same evidence. Consider the following example: in an early APL study, one of the awarding bodies identified a number of portfolios that had been assessed at Centre A towards a particular qualification. They then asked a group of equally trained assessors at Centre B to assess the same portfolios without knowledge of the decisions made by the assessors at Centre A. Once the portfolios were assessed by the second group, and the outcomes recorded, the awarding body research staff compared the results of the two assessments. They

---

* Prior to taking the UK driving test, of course, the driving candidate must complete a statement regarding his or her health, including any problems with vision. Some problems, such as night blindness, would lead to restrictions being placed on the driver.

were pleased to find a high level of agreement among the assessors regarding the decisions made about each portfolio, suggesting that the assessments were reliable.

In most norm-referenced assessment measures, reliabilities are presented as numerical indices linked to standard errors of measurement. In competence-based assessment there are usually no numerical indices since each assessment is based on the unique evidence presented by individual candidates, who work to predefined standards or learning outcomes. Non-numeric consistency of judgement is, perhaps, a more appropriate way of thinking about reliability in this context.

Sufficiency

As the word suggests, sufficiency relates to the *amount* of evidence needed during the assessment. It is impossible to give specific guidelines for sufficiency because in competence-based assessment the evidence submitted by each candidate varies considerably. However, prior to beginning their assessments, assessors should try to establish rough guidelines for themselves (and the advisors and candidates), anticipating not only the types of evidence candidates might bring forward but the nature and amount that would be most acceptable in light of the requirements of the standards or the learning outcomes. They may also find it helpful to speak with other professionals and awarding body representatives. Returning to the UK driving test, the practical part of the test is deemed not quite sufficient. And the oral questioning would fall far short of being sufficient. Trebling the time of the actual driving test to include motorway and night driving might provide sufficient evidence but at too high a cost. Extending the oral questioning would never make it sufficient (or valid). The current combination of the driving test *and* the oral questioning is assumed to provide sufficient evidence by which an assessor can judge whether or not an individual is competent to drive.

In constructing their portfolios, many adults tend to gather large amounts of the same type of evidence. They often believe that more is better. Flexible assessment providers who do not offer adequate guidelines to candidates on the nature of acceptable evidence should not be surprised to receive vast amounts of overlapping or irrelevant evidence. On-going discussion and information-sharing among advisors and assessors is essential.

Advisors or mentors need to help candidates select or generate the 'right' amount of evidence that will allow the assessors to complete the assessments. But it is the assessors who need to provide this information to the advisors either orally or, preferably, in writing. The advisors can then transmit the information to the candidates, either in the portfolio development workshops or in their one-to-one meetings. It is important to add that this information about assessment evidence will invariably change as assessors learn from experience about the evidence candidates can and do generate or bring forward in performance settings.

Authenticity

Authenticity was highlighted in the last chapter. Essentially it refers to the 'ownership' of the evidence. Can the assessor be sure that the evidence presented in the portfolio really does represent the achievements of the candidate submitting it? In flexible assessment the issue of authenticity is of special concern because often the assessor may meet the candidate only at the time of assessment or perhaps not at all! It is essential that assessors verify not only the evidence produced by the candidate but sometimes the indirect evidence as well.

Most often a particular portfolio, for example, will contain a range of evidence. This combination of evidence frequently serves to verify the authenticity of any particular piece of evidence. As will be discussed later, there are a number of other ways that assessors can also confirm the authenticity of the evidence.

Currency

The concept of currency refers to the recency of the evidence. Assessors must be sure that the evidence submitted by candidates is current enough to be considered appropriate to the assessment. There are a number of interesting issues that need to be addressed concerning currency. The currency questions candidates most frequently ask are:

- how recent is recent?
- may I use evidence from three, five, ten years ago?

Again, the answers to these questions must be determined by the assessors. It is they who must use the standards or learning outcomes to provide the best guidance they can to candidates and advisors. In competency-based systems candidates generally receive recognition or credit for what they know and can do *now*. The evidence, therefore, must relate to their current performance. High technology fields in which rapid change is expected may require candidates to present evidence that is no more than one or two years old. Other disciplines may easily allow older evidence. Older evidence, even in high technology fields, may provide valuable information to the assessor about a particular candidate's background and learning progression. It can serve to strengthen a candidate's more recent evidence and can provide a more complete picture of what a candidate really knows and can do.

In their review of portfolios and in offering guidance to candidates and advisors, it is essential that assessors consider these five principles of assessment. Carefully adhered to, assessors can be assured of both the rigour and the credibility of their assessment decisions.

Applying the principles to the review of diverse evidence

As the case studies in Chapter 4 illustrated, candidates may generate or produce diverse evidence in many different ways. Often, candidates will collect their evidence together in the form of a portfolio. Before submitting a portfolio for assessment, it is assumed that an advisor or an assessor has reviewed it for completeness and organisation, making sure that the evidence is properly cross-referenced and presented in a logical fashion.

The assessor's task then is to begin the assessment process. This is usually accomplished in a number of steps and can be interactive in nature, reflecting the candidate's progress and development over time.

1. *Familiarisation with the portfolio.* In some instances the assessor may actually have been serving as the advisor, in which case this step would not be required. However, an assessor new to a candidate's work will find that he or she needs to begin the process by skimming the portfolio – or other presentation of the evidence – to get an idea of what it contains. The assessor will want to read the personal report or narrative statement carefully in order to begin to understand the context(s) in which the candidate has been performing.

2. *Reviewing the evidence.* Using the cross-referencing form(s), the assessor reviews the actual evidence, making sure that it is relevant to the standards or learning outcomes (validity); that it represents sufficient breadth and quality to be appropriate to the standards to which it applies (sufficiency); that it is, beyond a reasonable doubt, the work of the candidate (authenticity); and that it is recent enough to meet the requirements of the performance criteria or learning outcomes (currency).

To undertake this review, many assessors find it useful to develop and ask a series of key questions for each piece of evidence:

- *Validity*
  Does the evidence relate to the standards or learning outcomes the candidate is claiming?
  Does it match in part or all of the standards within a particular unit?
- *Sufficiency*
  Can the evidence serve as conclusive proof for one or more of the units being assessed?
  If not, what else would be required?
- *Currency*
  Is the evidence sufficiently recent in light of the expectations of the standards?
- *Authenticity*
  Is the direct evidence definitely the work of the candidate?
  Does the indirect evidence provide a true and accurate picture to support the candidate's learning claim?

The answers to each of these, or similar, questions will help the assessor to judge each piece of evidence against the criteria specified by the standards. Of course for each 'no', the assessor will need to ask at least two other questions:

- What else do I need to know before I am satisfied that the candidate is competent or has achieved the claimed learning outcomes?
- What is the best way of obtaining the evidence required?

For example, it may be that the evidence presented by the candidate is somewhat relevant to the standards or learning outcomes but does not fully reflect what is being sought. Or it may be that the evidence is highly relevant but several years old. Or perhaps the nature of the indirect evidence is not strong enough to fully support some of the other evidence in the portfolio. Or maybe the candidate has little or no evidence because of the highly confidential nature of the candidate's work.

Each of these situations, and dozens more, will require the

assessor to develop a plan of action. This is called an assessment plan. If, on the other hand, the assessor believes that all of the criteria have been met and no further evidence is needed, the assessor can then recommend that the candidate receive the recognition or credit he or she is seeking.

The assessment plan

As assessors complete their reviews, they need to record their judgements and decisions. In so doing they create the assessment plan by which they will help the candidates collect or generate the necessary additional evidence that will enable the assessment to be completed. Several assessment options are available. These include: other artifacts or products; examples of indirect evidence; oral questioning; assignments or projects; demonstration; workplace assessment; or written tests. Figure 5.1, Assessor's Review Form, shows the way one organisation required the assessors to record the outcomes of their review of the portfolio and develop their initial assessment plans, which are then communicated and agreed with the candidates.

Additional artifacts or indirect evidence
Assessors frequently find that candidates can easily gather or produce additional artifacts that will satisfy the requirements of the assessment. This is one of the more expedient methods by which the assessment can be completed. Similarly, candidates may be able to request additional letters of validation or arrange for the assessor to speak with one or more of the people who have written on behalf of the candidate. In either case, the assessor needs to specify his or her request, give the candidate adequate time to produce the requested material and upon receipt of it continue with or complete the assessment.

In this context, letters of validation require highlighting. These letters can be essential to a candidate's learning claim, particularly when there are gaps in the evidence. They can serve to describe the context, provide details, or evaluate the candidate's strengths and weaknesses. Although it is the candidate's responsibility to request and obtain these letters, it is important

Unit title <u>Information Processing</u>   Candidate name <u>Claire Thompson</u>

Element of Competence 1:

Create a database file on commercially available software for recording, updating, manipulating and retrieving information.

Performance criteria

1

2

3

4

5

6

ASSESSOR'S REVIEW

Evidence assessed	Comments	Supplementary assessment recommended	Assessment completed
Evidence applicable to all performance criteria:			
Examples of work	Need to confirm currency	Oral questioning and/or demonstration	
Two letters of validation			
			Recommendation:
			Assessor's signature:
			Date:

Figure 5.1 *Assessor's Review Form*

Source: OU (1990) Unit 2, Module 2, p. 17.

for assessors to continually review the letters they receive and redefine what makes some letters stronger than others.

The more confidence assessors have in the letters they receive, the easier it will be to complete the candidate's assessment. After obtaining permission, therefore, the assessor should not hesitate to telephone the writer of a letter of validation to obtain additional information or to clarify particular issues.

Oral questioning

Oral questioning has several purposes. It can be used to:

- confirm current competence;
- test for knowledge and understanding that cannot be inferred from other evidence;
- clarify information;
- confirm important process skills only suggested by the evidence;
- authenticate evidence.

Oral questioning is used extensively in almost all competence-based assessment programmes. Often, candidates with their advisors and assessor elect early on to provide evidence through oral questioning, particularly to cover knowledge and understanding requirements. In addition, oral questioning can often provide an excellent assessment vehicle for people with literacy problems or for those whose cultures are more oriented to oral, rather than written, presentations.

Assignments or projects

In competence-based assessment systems, assignments and projects are used not just to generate assessment evidence but actively to promote learning and development. Assignments and projects – whether at work or in conjunction with education and training – should enable the candidate to demonstrate how he or she is able to integrate the standards or learning outcomes into their work and thinking. This can have spin-off benefits for employer organisations as well as for the individual candidates.

Often candidates are unable to identify evidence from past or current contexts to meet a particular standard or learning outcome. A specially designed assignment or project allows candidates to generate the evidence that will help them meet that requirement. Like all evidence, the outcomes of the assignment or project must reflect the standards, and candidates must be provided with the necessary specifications (length, size, time etc.) of the assignment or project. This form of assessment often plays a critical role for candidates with limited or no opportunities to gather or generate evidence from other sources.

Demonstration (including simulations and role play)
This form of assessment requires a special assessment occasion in which the assessor can observe the candidate performing a particular set of activities or skills. Assessors using one or more of these methods will need to make sure that the candidate is aware of both the standards or learning outcomes against which he or she is to be assessed and the circumstances under which the assessment is to be conducted (time, place, other participants, etc). The validity of these methods depends on how well the assessor designs them.

Unlike most of the other options open to assessors, demonstrations, simulations and role plays often require significant planning and the use of extensive resources. Care must be taken by assessors to balance the cost of conducting an assessment by demonstration with the validity of the evidence generated.

Workplace assessment
In most situations workplace assessments generate extremely valid evidence, particularly when the assessment takes place in the normal course of events and is conducted by an internal assessor.

Workplace assessments are particularly useful in competency-based systems or in flexible assessment programmes in which the best evidence is being generated by the candidate in his or her own place of work. As Docking (1990a) reports, workplace assessments can significantly reduce some of the problems created by other forms of assessment. For example, it is not necessary to 'simulate' or create an artificial environment in which to assess the candidate; there is no need to create a special reassessment opportunity if the first assessment does not go as planned; there also is an opportunity to observe the candidate integrating many different aspects of his or her performance which may not be easy to infer from other forms of assessment.

However, if the assessor is external to the workplace, a number of other issues arise:

- the candidate may be nervous and not perform as well;
- there may be organisational, health, safety or legal restrictions that will limit the assessor's accessibility to the candidate and detract from the validity of the assessment; and
- from the assessor's point of view, the time away from his or her normal workplace could create serious problems, not the least of which is cost.

Before agreeing to undertake assessments in the workplace, external assessors and their organisations will want to consider all of these factors. It may well be that if evidence is to be obtained from the workplace, the candidate will need to negotiate with his or her line manager to undertake an assessment and prepare a detailed letter of validation for the external assessor, who could then follow-up with minimal oral questioning, for example.

Written tests
Written tests may be useful when theories, knowledge or understanding cannot be inferred from other evidence. Although written tests are used extensively in traditional classrooms, flexible assessment assessors need to consider carefully issues of validity with such tests. Unless the assessor is assessing the candidate's writing performance, written examinations may not be appropriate – relevant – to the standards or learning outcomes.

In addition, it is important for assessors to remember that many adults will have been away from formal education and training for a long time. Since most will have been tested through written assessments, it is likely that many candidates will have a strong antipathy towards them and would prefer to be assessed by some other means if at all possible.

Recently some educational institutions have begun to think creatively about alternative evidence that could be used in place of conventional written assessments. Some examples are shown in Figure 5.2.

Obviously these various types of written work would need to relate to the standards, but just these few examples serve to illustrate the range of written evidence candidates can include in their portfolios which may lessen the need for the assessor to require additional written assessment.

Assessment options

Clearly the number of different assessment techniques an

Conventional assessment task	Alternative
Essay	Letter of advice to a Minister, a community action group or an employer. Magazine article prepared by the candidate. Book review prepared by the candidate.
Technical report	Tender for a contract.
Project report	Analysis of work problem with a written report.

Figure 5.2 *Alternative evidence*

111

assessor chooses to use will depend on a variety of factors. Most candidates' portfolios will contain a range of direct and indirect evidence and most assessors will use oral questioning for one purpose or another to supplement the initial evidence provided by the candidate. Ideally, it is most important for assessors to use the assessment techniques most appropriate to the needs of the individual candidates. For any given candidate, however, assessors should keep in mind that the range and quality of the evidence will vary considerably. Some candidates will be able to develop very strong portfolios that require no additional evidence or further assessment. At the other end of the spectrum will be candidates who have no products or even indirect evidence. These candidates will need to be assessed through one or more of the current assessment methods described above. And most candidates will fall somewhere in between, that is, they will have *some* evidence but will need to provide additional evidence or undergo further assessment to satisfy the expectations of the standards, and the assessor.

The important point here is that the process is led by the learner in response to the standards. Diverse evidence can be generated in many different ways and will reflect the particular context(s) unique to any given candidate. The diagram below illustrates the continuum of assessment – the toolbox from which all assessors and candidates can draw.

Organisational factors can also influence the choice of assessment options. Some of these include:

- the availability of resources;
- health and safety factors;
- time availability of candidates and assessors;
- competing roles, particularly for workplace assessors;
- accommodation for discussion and oral questioning;
- commitment of colleagues to provide witness testimonies or letters of validation;
- expertise to create role play or simulations.

Underpinning all of these factors, of course, is the one of cost.

CONTINUUM OF ASSESSMENT

Learning outcomes   Occupational standards

Assessment by portfolio

Assessment on demand

Course assessment   Workplace assessment

Demonstration   simulation or   project or   examination
                role play   assignment   – oral
                                                 – written

How much can an organisation afford to spend on the assessment process? On the other hand, can it afford not to invest fully in the development and assessment of its staff, trainees or students?

Pitfalls in assessment

Contrary to existing myths, assessment is not an exact science. Even so-called objective tests are still dependent on human judgement for both their development and scoring. Given that all assessment relies heavily on the decisions and judgements of assessors, it may be helpful to the potential assessor to be conscious of some of the more common assessment pitfalls (Stewart, 1990). By being more aware of them, assessors can strive to avoid them! There are several worth highlighting:

The halo effect. This is a common type of error in which the assessors makes the assumption that if one piece of evidence is good or bad, all the candidate's evidence will be equally good or bad.

113

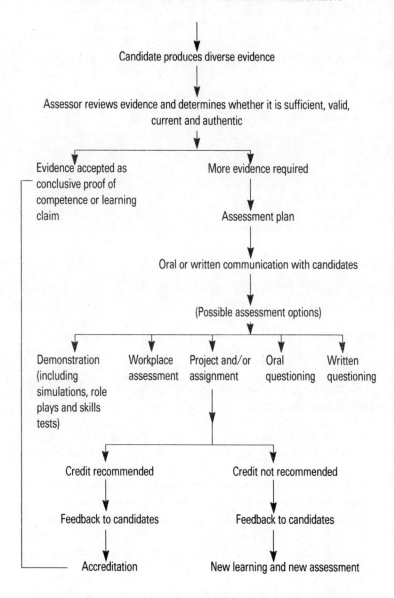

Figure 5.3 *Flowchart of the candidate-led assessment process*

First impressions. In this situation, the assessor uses the assessment process to confirm that his or her initial impressions were correct.

Contrast effect. This arises when the outcomes of an assessment are determined by comparing a particular candidate with a preceding one, whether good or bad.

Stereotyping. This refers to judgements made about a candidate based on presupposed characteristics of the individual and/or the evidence presented.

Similar to me. This occurs when a candidate or the evidence is judged favourably because the assessor perceives a strong similarity between the candidate and him- or herself.

Giving more weight to positives than to negatives. This may occur when a candidate's evidence or performance is contrary to what the assessor expects. This sometimes results in the assessor imposing unrealistic expectations on the candidate for the remainder of the assessment.

Experimenter effect. This occurs when the candidate performs or acts differently than would be expected because of the presence of the assessor. This effect is bound to be present to some degree in most assessment situations; it does not mean that the candidate's performance will be unacceptable.

Assessing progress rather than achievement. This occurs when the assessor pays too much attention to the effort or progress of a particular candidate, rather than to his or her attainments against the standards or learning outcomes. To the best of the assessor's ability, the candidate, and his or her evidence, should always be judged against the standards.

Lack of direction. In this instance assessors are not clear what it is they are assessing. It is important for assessors to be familiar with the standards or learning outcomes and know *in advance* the nature of the evidence or performance they are seeking.

Assessors answering their own questions. This occurs most often during oral assessments, particularly when assessors are not used to administering oral questions, are not familiar with the standards, or are uncomfortable in working with adults.

Illusion of validity. This occurs when the assessor feels good about his or her decision and therefore assumes it must be correct. However, this may mean that the assessor has found the evidence particularly interesting or the candidate particularly likeable rather than able.

Discriminatory practices. In assessment, as in other situations, this occurs when the assessor makes undue or unfair allowances or judgements for candidates because of race, gender, creed, sexual preference or special needs. Great care must be taken by assessors to make sure all candidates receive fair and equal opportunities during their assessments.

The assessor's role and responsibilities

In earlier chapters we reviewed and discussed the functions, roles and responsibilities of the advisors. It is important now to describe the roles and responsibilities of assessors. Thus far we have identified that the assessor has the prime responsibility for assessing candidates, determining whether or not they have met the standards or learning outcomes. But this is just one of the assessor's responsibilities. As specified by the Training and Development Lead Body, there are several functions assessors need to be able to carry out.

Unit D32 specifies that to assess a candidate's performance, the assessors should be able to:

- agree and review a plan for assessing performance;
- collect and judge performance evidence against criteria;
- collect and judge knowledge evidence; and
- make assessment decisions and provide feedback.

Unit D33 specifies that assessors need to be able to assess candidates using differing sources of evidence and that this requires them to:

- agree and review an assessment plan;
- judge evidence and provide feedback; and
- make assessment decisions using differing sources of evidence and provide feedback.

In establishing a sound flexible assessment system these are the competences required of all assessors.

Developing and using standards

Throughout this book continued reference has been made to standards or learning outcomes. They are the kingpin to sound assessments. Many professionals working in Britain use the National Vocational Qualifications (S/NVQ) framework which provides standards of occupational competence for a wide range of occupations. These standards have become part of normal training and educational provision and continue to serve as a basis for significant changes in the curriculum and in assessment methodology.

In the context of this book, the standards provide ready opportunities for adults who wish to earn one or more S/NVQs. Candidates, their advisors and assessors all have access to the standards. There are no hidden expectations lurking behind the minds of particular teachers or trainers. The standards are explicit, assessable, related to occupational competence and available for all to use. Assessments in the S/NVQ framework, therefore, have a clear focus: candidates are expected to prove their occupational competence as described by the units and elements of competence with their associate performance criteria.

Assessors working outside the context of S/NVQs, however, may find that there are no explicit standards or learning outcomes by which they can assess candidates. Although they may be recognising candidates' prior learning for purposes of access, exemption or placement, often their decisions are based more on 'gut feelings' or time-serving rather than explicit standards.

Professionals seriously wanting or needing to offer a sound assessment service need to begin by developing standards or learning outcomes (Simosko, 1988). This must be perceived as one of the primary responsibilities of assessors. Since they are the subject specialists, only they can develop the content specifications or standards. Through one method or another, they need to decide what is important about their discipline or occupation and from that spell out their expectations in the form of observable and assessable criteria. As summarised by Mitchell and Johnson (1987), 'Assessment is about generating evidence and making judgments (about) an individual's competence, by comparing his or her performance against established criteria'. Assessors working in environments or contexts that lack clear standards must lay the groundwork for their assessments by developing them.

Whether assessors are concerned with academic disciplines or occupational standards it is always possible to define the standards or expectations of the successful candidate. Often traditional educators argue that setting standards is acceptable for vocational areas but not for more theory-based fields; or they argue that a particular discipline is too complex to describe in terms of standards or learning outcomes. Yet every discipline and occupation *can* be analysed to develop clear, assessable standards. Knowledge, skills and understanding can all be articulated and assessed, at least to some degree. It may take time and patience to complete the analysis and develop the standards or learning outcomes, but it is possible. Professionals implementing flexible assessment services will need to explore one or more of the available methods by which to complete this work.

Providing feedback to candidates

Another primary responsibility of the assessor, as previously highlighted by the TDLB standards, is to provide feedback to candidates. This comes in at least two places in the assessment process: after the initial review of the portfolio and at the end of each completed assessment. Candidates need to be told what has been accepted and what more, if anything, is needed. They also need directions regarding any further assessments: they need to have a clear idea of what will be looked for during the assessment and what the particular situation will entail. Lastly, of course, they need to be advised of the outcome of the overall assessment.

Assessors should provide feedback as clearly and constructively as possible. As the standards state, 'feedback following the decision is clear, constructive, meets the candidate's needs and is appropriate to his/her level of confidence'. Even if the evidence in a portfolio is not sufficient or does not meet other technical requirements, the assessor should acknowledge that for most candidates the production of the portfolio represents a considerable amount of time, effort and emotional investment. Assessors should try to convey their respect for the effort of the candidate even when the evidence is lacking in one or more ways.

Similarly, at the end of any particular current assessment or at the end of the overall assessment period, if the candidate has not proved that he or she has met the standards or learning outcomes, the assessor must convey the news, but in a way that will encourage the candidate rather than undermine his or her continued efforts. In 'putting the customer first', assessors may need to remind themselves that the primary purpose of learner-centred assessment is to promote the development of the individual – to help him or her reach an important goal. Because a candidate was not successful in his or her attempt to receive the sought recognition or credit does not mean that the candidate should be deflected from continuing to work toward the desired goal. The way in which assessors provide feedback will be critical to how candidates feel about the overall process and often themselves. Assessors should therefore carefully consider the way in which they provide feedback to candidates. In this context it is especially important that assessors demonstrate a lack of bias or discrimination.

Maintaining records

Another responsibility of assessors is to prepare and maintain records for each assessment they complete. Again, this is spelled out in the standards as 'evidence and assessment decisions are recorded to meet verification requirements' and 'records are legible and accurate, stored securely and passed to the next stage of recording/certification process promptly'. This will involve recording the outcomes of the review of the portfolio and any subsequent assessment. It may also require the assessor to tape-record and store the outcomes of any oral assessments. Since assessors are very much a part of the overall quality assurance process, their records must be clear, accurate and complete for every candidate they assess.

Communicating with other professionals

Another essential responsibility of the assessor is to communicate effectively on a regular basis with a range of other professionals. These include the advisors, other assessors, internal or external verifiers, and administrative or management staff.

Advisors

Since it is the advisors who support candidates throughout the assessment process, it is essential that they are as well informed as possible. Assessors must therefore make sure that they meet and talk with the advisors on an on-going basis to keep them well briefed and to provide an opportunity to discuss particular issues or concerns. The better prepared the advisors are, the more likely it is that assessors will receive well organised and stronger portfolios and candidates who understand the nature of evidence and the expectations of any further assessments.

Assessors need to remember that in most contexts advisors are not technical experts. They cannot and do not make technical or academic judgements. However, with support from the assessors, they can go a long way in helping candidates interpret the standards, select or generate evidence and meet the overall requirements of the assessment.

The advisor may also wish the assessor to participate in either an orientation session or a portfolio development workshop. In these instances the advisor and the assessor will need to agree the exact role and contribution expected of the assessor.

It is important to add that in many contexts the roles of the advisor and the assessor are being integrated, particularly in workplace situations in which the supervisor or manager regularly observes the candidate's performance. In this context the assessment process is ongoing and a natural outcome of the candidate's development and performance at work.

Other assessors

Communication with other assessors either from within the same centre or across centres is also essential to a strong and credible flexible assessment programme. Assessors need to learn from one another: they need to know that they are interpreting the standards in a similar fashion, that they agree on the nature of acceptable evidence, and that they are meeting the needs of individual candidates in similarly effective and sensitive ways.

It is also useful for assessors to meet other assessors from different disciplines or occupational areas. The cross fertilisation that occurs frequently provides new information, perspective, and problem-solving techniques. Many assessors from both the workplace and from academic organisations find that meeting with subject specialists from other disciplines fosters self-confidence, stimulates thinking and encourages creativity.

Internal or external verifiers

Assessors need to provide information and feedback to both internal and external verifiers as part of the quality assurance process. Similarly, verifiers should expect to provide constructive feedback to assessors. The primary purpose of the verifiers is to ensure that the standards have been met; that the assessments have been conducted in a fair and reliable way; and that any outstanding issues regarding the specifications or interpretation of the standards are identified. Assessors and verifiers need to work together to make sure these things happen.

Administrators and managers
Both college and work-based assessors usually have to provide updates to administrators or managers who want to know how the assessment process is working. Assessors therefore will want to collect relevant information about candidate progress, the nature of evidence, units assessed and any number of other things – including budgets and bottom-line benefits! – that may be relevant to the management of the service. Keeping clear and accurate records and working closely with advisors, other assessors and verifiers will help each assessor to meet the administrative and management needs of his or her organisation.

The role and responsibilities of assessors may vary in degree from one organisation to another. However, in all contexts assessors will be expected to meet a range of technical and communication requirements and should be prepared to respond to the needs of individual candidates, colleagues, and their own organisations.

Summary

Sound assessments are critical to the development of a flexible assessment service. Assessors must adhere to a range of principles of good practice. These include making sure the evidence submitted and/or generated by candidates is valid, reliable, sufficient, authentic and recent enough to be of value to the assessment.

As part of their review of diverse evidence, assessors will need to develop assessment plans for each candidate and convey to candidates either orally or in writing the outcomes of the assessment. Following the review of the initial diverse evidence, assessors may need to ask candidates to generate additional evidence through oral questioning, demonstrations or other techniques. In conducting these assessments, assessors must be wary of a range of assessment pitfalls.

The assessor's role and responsibilities extend beyond assessing candidates. In some cases assessors may need to develop standards or learning outcomes and always they will be expected to give constructive feedback to candidates, maintain records, and communicate with other professionals about their work.

Chapter 6

Implementing Assessment Services

Thus far we have looked at the purpose and benefits of flexible assessment and the key roles and responsibilities of advisors and assessors. In this chapter we will investigate implementation issues, those concrete, practical issues that must be addressed before a sound service can be introduced. Many organisations find that flexible assessment services can be integrated easily into their normal provision; others find that the integration itself acts as a catalyst for much needed change.

The suggestions offered here are not intended to be prescriptive – because every organisation has its own distinct needs and ways of doing things – but, as Rosabeth Moss Kanter (1985) suggests, there is a lot organisations can learn from the innovation and success of others. This chapter is based largely on the experiences of dozens of organisations in both Britain and North America that have developed strong, exciting competence-based programmes that have served not only the learning and development needs of the adults making use of the service but the needs and interests of the organisation as well. In the UK, of course, much innovation and success has taken place in the context of introducing S/NVQs, particularly in the workplace.

Organisational purpose

A college, university, employer or other training provider wishing to introduce flexible assessment services should carefully consider its reason for wanting to do so. Does it want to:

- improve performance?
- motivate individuals better?
- attract new employees, students or trainees?
- introduce new learner-driven services?
- make better use of existing learning and training provision?
- develop new partnerships with other organisations?

All of these are examples of why some organisations have chosen to develop and introduce flexible assessment services. They have identified an organisational need that they felt could be met by introducing new strategies for developing and assessing people. But it is one thing to *want* to do something and quite another to actually do it. For many organisations the bridge between the two is often an over-arching review or organisational audit. This self-assessment allows the organisation to analyse its mission, policies and procedures and, from that, develop an institutional action plan which will facilitate the introduction of flexible assessment with its incumbent services and structures.

Flexible assessment services and the organisational audit

As we have seen throughout this book, the concept of flexible assessment – and with it APL – is based on several assumptions which frequently do not characterise traditional education and training programmes. It requires a different emphasis within the organisation and the roles and functions of staff can differ significantly. Some examples of these differences are shown in Figure 6.1.

Once organisations realise that some of the requirements of

Traditional	Flexible assessment
• Organisation provides *learning* and assessment opportunities.	• Organisation provides *assessment* and learning opportunities.
• Policies and procedures often based on historical justifications and administrative convenience.	• Policies and procedures based on needs of learners within constraints of the organisation.
• Assessment is linked to particular learning or training programme.	• Assessment is not linked to any particular learning or training programme.
• Subject specialist is first and foremost a teacher.	• Subject specialist is first and foremost an assessor.
• No necessary separation of advising, teaching and assessing roles.	• Separation of advising, teaching and assessing roles, as appropriate.

Figure 6.1 *Differences between traditional and flexible assessment educational and training programmes*

flexible assessment differ from those of their normal delivery system, they begin to see the need for the institutional audit.

A sound audit will investigate how well the organisation is placed for delivering flexible learning and assessment services. This will include a thorough analysis of:

- organisational mission and business objectives and strategies;
- the premises and accommodation;
- the written and visual information available;
- development needs of the staff;

- the organisation and availability of learning, training and assessment services;
- the nature of the individuals making use of the services;
- the framework by which learners progress through the system;
- costs and fees and;
- the management structure.

By looking at each of these and learning from the experience of others, professionals wanting to implement flexible assessment will have some guidance as to how to proceed.

What follows is a brief analysis of each of these areas, highlighting key factors that potential providers need to consider. A list of questions has also been developed to help the reader design and conduct his or her own organisational audit. Although the type and range of questions an organisation might ask itself will vary, those presented suggest useful areas for exploration. From the outcomes of the audit, a centre can develop its own implementation or action plan for introducing – or improving – its flexible learning and assessment services.

Missions, business objectives and strategies

Today almost all organisations have mission statements and increasingly clear business objectives and strategies. Both have become survival tools to communicate to external customers and internal staff the purpose of the organisation and its objectives. This is true in both business and industry environments as well as in education and training contexts. However, as organisations contemplate major change and innovation, reviewing and modifying the mission statement and business objectives and strategies can sometimes play a significant role in preparing people to adapt to new ways of working or thinking. This has been true in many instances as the introduction of S/NVQs has progressed in the UK, and as new approaches to learning and development have been implemented in colleges and universities around the world. By way of example, one college in North America discovered that its mission statement had not been reviewed or changed in ten years. The original statement reflected the college's purpose which was basically to attract and educate traditional-aged students right out of high school for the primary purpose of equipping them to become 'better citizens'. In the course of the ten years, however, many changes had taken place within the college, largely as a result of significant demographic changes in the area. The college now enrolled as many people over the age of 25 as it did those under 25 and a large percentage of its resources was spent on meeting the basic skills needs of a significant population of new immigrants. It also offered a wide variety of vocational programmes, unknown ten years ago.

In this particular case, the lack of an appropriate mission statement did not undermine the college's ability to respond effectively to changing circumstances. But not all organisations are so lucky. The lack of an appropriate mission statement may not only limit the organisation's ability to attract the customers it wants, it may also contribute to on-going debate among staff as to what they should be doing in their jobs.

The changing role of further education in the UK provides an apt example of this. Ten years ago further education colleges served basically two purposes: (1) to support apprenticeship training programmes and (2) to deliver full-time courses for those school leavers unable to get into higher education. The current-day structures and policies of many colleges are still geared to meeting these purposes. Yet regularly colleges are finding that they must meet the needs of increasingly diverse populations, including more adult returners; that people want greater flexibility in both learning and assessment opportunities; that local employers expect the college to deliver a range of short courses; S/NVQs must be offered alongside more traditional qualifications; and all the while colleges are being expected to operate increasingly on a full-cost recovery basis. It is no wonder that staff – managers, lecturers, and support staff – often feel overwhelmed and confused.

The more innovative colleges are taking a hard look at what

they *can* and *want* to deliver and are identifying their primary client groups. From that they are developing sound mission statements to describe their purposes, roles and ultimate objectives. These statements – hopefully developed and agreed by large numbers of the staff – serve as the primary vehicles by which the college lets its various customers (potential clients, employers, awarding bodies and others) learn about its objectives and commitments.

Employers also continue to review and modify their mission statements with an increasing awareness of meeting the needs of not just their external customers but the internal ones too – the staff. They have found that by introducing comprehensive learning and assessment opportunities based on the national standards for staff, they are better able to fulfill their mission to external customers and increase profitability and effectiveness.

In the context of flexible assessment services, which are highly learner-centred, the organisation's mission statement ideally should embrace the notion of facilitating the development of each individual it serves; of providing flexible learning and assessment opportunities; and of delivering a range of integrated, complementary programmes designed to meet the needs of particular client and/or employee groups.

Case Study

Consider The ACE Conveyor Equipment, a UK-based company, that achieved ISO9000 and the Investors in People (IIP) award. As part of their effort to work towards IIP, they encouraged every employee to gain an NVQ with ongoing training, support and flexible assessment available to all employees. As part of its evaluation, the company found many benefits: staff motivation increased; staff turnover was reduced; learning and training became an accepted part of the culture; the 'new attitude towards training . . . underlined the belief that employees are the company's biggest asset'.

Selected Questions

1. Does the organisation have a clear, up-to-date mission statement?
2. If you represent a college or training provider, does your mission statement reflect an orientation that includes adults?
3. If you represent an employer organisation, does your mission statement reflect a commitment to develop *all* of your employees?
4. Do your business objectives and strategies clearly support your mission statement?

Premises and accommodation

In education and training contexts, part of the audit must also look at the nature of the physical plant in which the flexible assessment service is to be located. Many centres take their premises for granted and do not realise how inhospitable they often have become. Vast resources are often spent on keeping places looking cold and uninviting. One college principal was astounded at the initial reluctance of staff to the suggestion that students' art work be displayed around the college, not just in the corridors near the art department. Staff long-accustomed to the barren off-white walls (which were regularly painted and maintained) argued that: 'students will deface the art work'; 'hanging the pictures will be expensive'; 'the stuff isn't that good'; 'this isn't a museum, it's a college!' But the principal's decision prevailed. The art and design students organised the display of the work as an extension or their on-going classroom work; staff and students alike were amazed at the high level of creativity and diversity of the work; and after several months, staff and visitors alike looked forward to the changing 'show'.

This is but one small example of the way in which one education centre began to make its environment more friendly and welcoming. By displaying the students' art work the college was publicly supporting its mission statement by saying that people count and that the organisation valued the diversity of its contributing members.

Why, you may be asking, is this so critical to the success of flexible assessment services? The reason is simple: the environment offered by an organisation is one of the most important outward manifestations of its mission statement. An organisation committed to fostering the development of individuals needs to welcome those individuals and make them feel that the place itself is there to be *used* and *enjoyed*. It is not a prison; people, especially adults, come there of their own volition. All too many centres professing a commitment to learner-centredness do little to demonstrate this commitment in their premises.

If we remember earlier discussions about candidates, many of whom carry long-standing fears and hostilities about education, training and assessment, it becomes the centre's responsibility to make sure those people are treated in a way that will facilitate their progression. One way to do that is to make sure the environment is inviting and comfortable.

When asked what they liked most about the physical environment of their colleges or training organisations, adults from several different nations representing various levels and contexts of education and training have said:

- There were clear directions to everything I needed.
- Parking was available.
- When I first went in I was pleased to see plants and pictures. It wasn't anything like I expected.
- It was bright and airy. I didn't feel closed in.
- The information I needed was right where my advisor said it would be.
- The receptionist smiled and seemed genuinely friendly.
- I chose my centre because it has child-minding facilities.
- Everyone's name is visible when you go into the office.

Except for the parking and child-minding facilities, none of these observations required a large outlay of money by the providing organisation, yet all contributed to making the adults (and no doubt others) feel welcome. These comments, and

131

others like them, reflect a belief among candidates that they selected the right place for the help and services they required.

Selected Questions

1. Are key offices well sign-posted outside and inside the building(s)?
2. Is there adequate parking and/or public transport when the centre is open?
3. Are the interiors of the buildings light, airy and well ventilated?
4. Is access available to all offices, toilets and other facilities for people with special needs?
5. Have receptionists, security guards and others been trained to greet and respond to the questions of potential candidates?
6. Are facilities open and staffed in the evenings and at the weekends?

Written and visual material

When the concept of APL was first introduced, the words themselves – the accreditation of prior learning – became an accepted part of education and training jargon. However, as use and applications developed, the words gradually shifted as providers recognised that APL as a stand-alone product or service had no real meaning for most people. In its place new concepts, broader in scope and more meaningful to larger numbers of people, were introduced. In many cases this reflected a strong desire to de-jargonise the language and to put assessment services right where they belong: in the centre of learning and development programmes.

Based on this experience, a centre wanting to introduce the concept of APL as part of its flexible assessment services should plan to conduct a review of its written and visual material. It should make sure that the tone, clarity and visual presentation of the materials reflect the mission of the organisation and the needs of the individuals likely to make use of the service. Many employer organisations have found that they need to 'translate' jargon-ridden publications and forms from education and training providers to make them accessible and understandable to their workforces. A careful review and appropriate revision of education and training materials could avoid this time-consuming and expensive activity for employer organisations.

Although many aspects of the audit can be well conducted by groups of staff members across the institution, the review of the written and visual materials often requires the involvement of outsiders as well. Those within a given organisation may see nothing 'wrong' or misleading about particular words, phrases, or visual images because they have been so close to it for a long period of time. It often takes the views of outsiders to highlight the inadequacies of publications.

This review does not always require the outside expertise of a professional editor or consultant. Many flexible assessment centres (and other truly learner-centred organisations) request on-going feedback from their various client groups to make sure the language of their publications is relevant to the needs and aspirations of particular client groups, understandable, and non-discriminatory. Properly designed questionnaires, completed by candidates (whether students, trainees or employees), can provide valuable information which will enable a centre to revise, modify or do away with some aspects of its publications or other visual materials.

Selected Questions

1. Do the visual images of publications reflect the diversity of the various client groups served by the organisation?
2. Are the words used jargon-free and easy to understand?
3. Is regular feedback from candidates collected, analysed and used to modify materials?
4. Is there an internal editorial committee or board which meets regularly to review and update the materials of the organisation?

Skills and training needs of staff

In the UK, advisors and assessors need to be accredited with the appropriate TDLB units. All across the nation and in most occupations, employers and education and training providers alike are investing significant time and effort to help individuals achieve these units. Almost all organisations, however, will find that they need to make sure the staff have the skills and knowledge necessary to provide flexible assessment services. They will probably need to conduct an 'audit' of their staff. This doesn't mean just tallying up the number of degrees and other qualifications of the staff. It means taking a hard look at the particular skills and strengths of the staff and from that determining further training needs.

For example, almost all teachers and trainers, regardless of the level or context in which they work, do assessment. Yet very few have had any formal training as assessors. Teacher training programmes may include some input on assessment, but only rarely is assessment conceived of as something more than written tests designed to test candidates' or students' knowledge. Very few people in education or business contexts have been trained to consider a diversity of evidence in their assessments; even fewer have been trained to use standards or learning outcomes as the basis of their assessments. Indeed experience suggests that there is a genuine lack of understanding about the basic principles of assessment and that much of the assessment candidates are subjected to is based on a strong set of myths (Docking, 1990b). For example, many traditional subject specialists who teach or train really believe the following:

Myth: That assessment must be a competitive process, pitting one learner against another, and that collaborative effort is tantamount to 'cheating'.

Myth: That the excellence of the few can only be attested by the failure of the many.

Myth: That assessment should be a retrospective, summative and terminating process.

Myth: That grades (A, B, C, D; deciles; percentiles, etc) can faithfully and meaningfully reflect performance in a unit of study or over a collection of units.

Myth: That assessment processes must be hidden and secret from the learner (and often the trainer) if fairness is to be ensured.

Myth: That knowledge alone can be an adequate indicator of real performance.

Myth: That assessment methods should be devised to heighten the fear of failure and the hope of success as motivating strategies for comprehensive and effective learning.

Myth: That anxiety and pain are necessary accompaniments to rigorous assessment.

All of these myths – so deeply believed by many professional educators and trainers – are contrary to the successful implementation of competence-based assessment systems. Staff need ongoing support and development to see the assessment process in new ways.

Experience suggests that if large numbers of staff do not think that flexible assessment will work, it won't!

Although this example has focused on the area of assessment, a similar example could be developed about advising or managing the service. Simply by way of example, many highly trained advisors in colleges and universities think it is their job to tell candidates what to do: they tell them what courses to take, which lecturer they might find best, what qualification to seek. Flexible assessment advisors, on the other hand, must be willing to give control to the learner and provide on-going support and guidance as necessary. Many advisors, long accustomed to working with young people, find it difficult at first to actually negotiate fully with the adults they meet. Once they do, of course, they often report much higher job satisfaction since frequently the interactions with the flexible assessment candidates are so positive.

Similarly many managers believe that to manage properly

they must distance themselves from those on their teams. The delivery of flexible assessment requires close team work between the advisors, assessors and managers. More effective managers regularly provide team-building opportunities for their staff.

The audit, then, needs to identify the technical strengths the staff could bring to the service. Because the process can represent such a radical departure from the way much traditional assessment works, it must also reveal staff willingness to try something new – be that working with adults or colleagues in new ways.

Selected Questions

1. Have subject specialists been trained and/or accredited to use a variety of evidence in their assessments?
2. Have all staff been trained to develop and/or use standards of competence or learning outcomes?
3. Do staff regularly work with adults or will they need orientation to the needs of adults?
4. Are advisors trained to lay out options and give candidates control of their own decisions?
5. In workplace contexts, do sufficient numbers of staff have mentoring skills?
6. Do staff participate in regular, on-going team-building exercises?
7. Is professional development about flexible assessment and related initiatives made available to staff and is it properly resourced?

Supporting candidates

Flexible assessment services must be prepared to provide a wide variety of support to candidates, recognising that some will require more than others. The audit needs to identify the range of ways that candidates can receive advising, learning and assessment services as part of a coherent, learner-centred framework.

In Chapters 3 and 4 we looked at the range of services offered by advisors. But the audit needs to look at the structure in which the advisors function, the range of other responsibilities they have and the time allocated to deliver the service. All too often centres embark on flexible assessment services without careful consideration of these issues and find they have created an organisational nightmare for the staff and the candidates.

Candidates frequently express frustration and dissatisfaction if they are unable to reach their advisors on a regular basis. Increasingly, however, many education and training providers are reallocating the time of their staff to include advising and assessment responsibilities in addition to those related to instruction.

Each institution will need to consider carefully how best to provide the ongoing support candidates need. Many different models exist: in some education and training organisations advisors are 'generalists', not linked to any particular department or occupational area. In others they are subject specialists, sometimes also serving as assessors. In workplace contexts sometimes the supervisor is both mentor and assessor; in others these functions are separated. More essential than any particular role, however, the organisation needs to determine the range of services required by its candidate groups and then ensure that:

- staff are trained and/or accredited to deliver those services;
- learners understand the options available to them;
- the roles and responsibilities of everyone are clearly defined; and
- the service is monitored and evaluated on an on-going basis.

Thus far in this book we have said little about new learning. Yet for many candidates the acquisition of new skills and knowledge is critical to their overall development plans. They want to receive recognition or credit for what they already know and can do, so that they can get on to something else. In Britain as in certain quarters in North America the issue of providing new learning has been one of the biggest impediments to the

137

implementation of flexible assessment services, primarily because the educational structure is not sufficiently flexible to allow learners to gain the 'bits and pieces' of new learning they may require to complete a unit or qualification.

Ideally all centres offering flexible assessment should have a unitised or modularised curriculum which will allow candidates to drop in and out as needed. They should also offer a range of open or distance learning options and should be able to offer flexible workshops which will help candidates 'top up' on an informal basis. But this is the ideal and in most contexts very far from the reality and constraints of education-based centres. Industrial training organisations and employers often do have modularised training with distance or open learning components but, as would be expected, these offerings are not always in the areas needed or wanted by the candidate.

The implementation of NVQs in England, Wales and Northern Ireland, and National Certificates and SVQs in Scotland has eased the situation only slightly. Largely because of financial and administrative concerns, many FE colleges continue to offer one- or two-year S/NVQ courses. However, examples of flexible and cost effective learning opportunities do continue to emerge, albeit slowly. Open and distance learning opportunities have developed to help compensate for the lack of responsiveness in some colleges. Sometimes, however, these are expensive and indeed are not always appropriate for some learners who are 'returning to learning', and require more in-person support and motivation.

Employers also need to consider how best to provide flexible learning opportunities. In conjunction with S/NVQs, of course, much development takes place at work. However, sometimes individuals require additional learning opportunities – training, new assignments, special projects, etc.

In North America the credit-hour system does provide for considerable modularisation when compared with the British system. But even there, the issue arises: since flexible assessment services are offered primarily in colleges and universities and often, it must be said, without benefit of clear standards or learning outcomes, candidates frequently have heavy knowledge and understanding assessments to undergo. Although many adults are rich in experience and indeed would far exceed the performance of recent graduates, they often lack the required text-book theory material that is so deeply entrenched in North American higher education. One college in the Midwest received federal support to offer only the theory-based material of a range of traditional courses. Candidates could come in the evenings for the segments they felt they needed during the time they were developing their portfolios. By the time they were ready to undergo assessment, most felt adequately prepared to take the knowledge-based assessments. As valuable as the programme was, however, regrettably the college was not able to sustain it once the initial funding was exhausted.

One model which seems to overcome many of the obstacles of further and higher education can be found in some of the more innovative centres in Britain. Many offer the same qualifications as traditional colleges but do so in a way that is both flexible and efficient. Trainees are assessed before they receive training so that both the trainee and the trainers know in advance what his or her other strengths are. Then, because the delivery is already modularised and delivered in on-going workshops, candidates can attend only those sessions they need to meet the requirements of the full qualification.

The area of providing new learning will be a challenge to most readers of this book. And indeed, professionals throughout the world are addressing many of these, and other, issues. Many flexible assessment providers are seeking new partnerships in an attempt to come up with positive solutions. As the total quality management example in Chapter 2 demonstrates, partnerships may be the most useful way forward in this area. Certainly in the UK, consortia of employers – sometimes in partnership with colleges – have proved effective. Under these arrangements, companies share training resources and on-the-job opportunities in order to provide diverse learning opportunities to employees. In education, training and workplace environments, far greater use is also being made of technology, including the Internet, to maximise learning options.

Centres deciding to offer flexible assessment services should at least be clear on the available options they can offer candidates. Again, the audit should serve to highlight both the strengths of any given institution and also its limitations.

Assessment services need to be delivered in a flexible manner, and at times convenient to both candidates and assessors. Experience suggests that unless assessors are properly resourced they often find that other professional, managerial and technical responsibilities come before their assessment work.

What has become obvious in recent years is that to deliver an effective flexible assessment service, the roles of traditional educators and trainers need to be modified. This is also true in employment contexts where some roles need to be widened to encompass the functions and activities of assessors and/or mentors. Once the roles are more clearly described and agreed with the staff (and sometimes local government organisations, unions, and others), it becomes much easier to *reallocate* resources. The implementation of flexible assessment and other learner-centred services may not require more money but it will most assuredly require a different distribution.

Selected Questions

1. Are staff and candidates clear about the way in which portfolios, the outcomes of assessment and candidate records are processed and maintained?
2. Are candidates able to make use of a wide variety of learning resources, including distance and open learning, flexible workshops, or individualised learning programmes?
3. Are partnerships in place whereby the organisation can cost-effectively increase its new-learning options to candidates?
4. Are new-learning options available in the evenings and/ or at weekends?
5. Is technology being used as effectively as it might to increase learning opportunities?

6. Are professional staff given time to develop the materials they need to support adults wanting or needing new learning?

Nature of learners

Whether in education, training or employment contexts, more organisations will need to think about the nature of the individuals who will be making use of the service. As previously highlighted, different learners have different needs. The most effective organisations systematically determine the likely strengths and limitations of any particular group of candidates, trainees or employees in order to modify or introduce appropriate services. For example, experienced working managers might require very different services than semi-skilled unemployed people. The former might be able to take significant responsibility for generating diverse evidence using written materials alone; the latter might require more one-to-one support. The audit should help organisations clarify the needs of all the diverse learners they hope to serve effectively.

Selected Questions

1. Do recruitment efforts aim at groups of people as reflected in the mission statement?
2. Have materials been designed to attract or retain adults?
3. Has the organisation formed partnerships with other organisations in an effort to attract candidates who could most benefit from the service?
4. Are regular orientation sessions or workshops held in the community to provide potential candidates with information about flexible assessment and other learner-centred services?
5. Is there systematic follow-up of all people who contact the organisation but do not progress?
6. In employment contexts, have the support needs of all the different learner groups been identified?

Framework by which learners progress through the system

Organisations considering flexible assessment should remember that the basic purpose is to facilitate the progression of individuals. To that end, the organisation needs to try to simplify its procedures and reduce red tape. This is often easier said than done! But the audit should reveal the points of tension between the needs of individuals and the needs of the administrative structure.

Clearly stated policies can go a long way to help candidates *and staff* understand the flexible assessment model once in place. A flexible assessment organisation needs to have policies in place regarding:

- fees;
- top-up learning;
- acceptable assessment options;
- time frame for portfolio development;
- nature (and in some contexts amount) of credit that can be awarded;
- appeals procedures; and
- type of records retained about each candidate.

These policies should be consistent with other policies developed by the organisation and should not in any way marginalise either the staff who deliver the services or the candidates themselves. The process works best when it is integrated with other programmes and services an organisation may offer. The audit should serve to reveal where flexible assessment easily 'fits' and where modifications are needed to existing policies.

Selected Questions

1. Is the fee structure clear, easy to understand and fair in light of other charges the centre makes?
2. Are policies clear and precise as to the nature and amount of credit candidates can earn?

3. Are new-learning options provided at times and in a manner needed by candidates?
4. Are time frames set and agreed with staff and candidates?
5. Is there a sound appeals process in place?
6. Are the records developed and maintained for each candidate clear and in keeping with all legislation regarding the confidentiality of data?

Costs and fees

Resourcing flexible assessment is another key factor in its implementation. Organisations will need to review and analyse all relevant cost factors in order to develop a strategy for setting fees. Experience has shown that there are different cost features related to the start-up of the service and the actual offering of the service.

For example, during the start-up phase the centre may need to consider staff development, professional advice/support, technical expertise, the production of materials, the purchase of equipment, and accommodation. Some of these cost features, however, may already be paid for by one or more other programmes or services, eg, equipment and accommodation. So the audit will need to determine what *new* costs will be associated with the development of a flexible assessment service.

The costs associated with the delivery of the service will also need to be analysed. These include:

- the staffing of the service, eg advisor(s), assessor(s), manager or coordinator, and support staff;
- accommodation, eg, advising area(s), assessment area(s), storage area(s) and any newly created open learning area;
- equipment;
- consumables, eg, telephone, postage, forms, tapes, other printed matter like brochures and guides for candidates;
- marketing or promotion materials, including items for briefing and portfolio development workshops; and
- external validation and/or verification.

143

Not included in this list is the provision of new-learning opportunities because it is assumed that these options will be drawn on by a range of learners, not just the flexible assessment candidates.

Many employers carry out cost-benefit analyses. Often they find that start-up costs can be high but are outweighed by the long-term benefits to their employees. In education and training contexts too, financial analyses are often carried out: not just in the context of flexible assessment services but in an effort to modularise the curriculum, modify the roles and responsibilities of staff, introduce technology, improve support services and streamline administrative procedures. In this context, flexible assessment is but one cost factor that providing institutions need to consider.

Selected Questions

1. Has the centre developed a flexible assessment model and identified the cost factors associated with each?
2. Has the centre compared possible costs and fees of flexible assessment with those of other services and programmes of the centre?
3. Is the pricing structure based on sound reasoning and consistent with candidates' ability to pay?

The management structure

Once again, the audit needs to dip into a sensitive area, that of the management structure! For flexible assessment to work effectively, it must be delivered through an effective team approach and the management of both the organisation and the service itself should reflect the values conveyed in the mission statement.

Increasingly colleges, universities, training organisations and employers are exploring the ideas of Total Quality Management (TQM), the Learning Organisation and Investors in People (IIP) as was briefly mentioned in Chapter 2. Interest in these seems to reflect a growing need within organisations to make staff more

144

responsive not just to the requirements of the external customers or clients but to the needs of the staff as internal customers
as well. Since the success of the assessment service – and any
other learner-centred service – is so dependent on effective team
work, managers offering assessment and related services need to
encourage mutual respect, interdependence and effective communication among all staff.

The placement of the flexible assessment service within an
organisation can have a significant impact on the type of
management that is possible. As is stated throughout this book,
flexible assessment services need to be integrated with other
learning and assessment services or opportunities. They cannot
be placed peripherally within an organisation, otherwise both
staff and candidates may feel like 'second-class citizens'.
Management and staff alike should perceive that flexible
assessment is but *one* option that will help facilitate the
progression of individuals. It is by no means the *only* means of
assisting learners and for that reason works most effectively in
the context of a range of other services and programmes.

Selected Questions

1. Are managers within the organisation committed to team
   building and some of the notions of TQM, the Learning
   Organisation or IIP?
2. Does the structure of the organisation enable everyone to
   see their role as equal to, if different from, those of their
   colleagues?
3. Is the service appropriately linked to other programmes
   and services within the organisation?
4. Do advisors, assessors, and support staff regularly meet
   with one another and the manager?
5. Does the manager foster regular and on-going
   communication with others in the centre?

Monitoring and evaluating the service

Monitoring and evaluating the flexible assessment service are critical activities that should be conducted on a regular basis. Because success is so dependent on maintaining the clarity and effectiveness of each stage in the process, the quality of the monitoring and evaluation will require the involvement of everyone connected with the service: advisors, assessors, support staff, managers and of course the candidates themselves.

Monitoring involves checking the on-going quality of the service. 'Formative evaluation' is another way of describing the monitoring process. Is the service, for example, meeting the standards and expectations of those who make use of it and those who contribute to it? To monitor a service effectively, the providing centre needs

- to identify what regular, on-going information needs to be collected, and
- to set performance indicators so that the information collected can be judged against these indicators.

Monitoring and evaluation require the collection, analysis and interpretation of information to determine whether the service or programme is meeting its overall objectives. In the context of flexible assessment, monitoring and evaluating are most often geared to *improving* the service for subsequent candidates, the staff who provide the service and the organisation itself.

Designing the evaluation

There are several different types of evaluation: quantitative, qualitative and goal-free.

- Quantitative is based on the collection of precise information; for example, the number of people completing the assessment process or the number of credits awarded.

- Qualitative is based on the views and opinions of people involved in the process; for example, the feedback candidates might provide about the advisory services.
- Goal-free evaluation involves an unstructured approach which assumes no pre-conditions of information. A discussion or interview about the need for the service would be an example of a goal-free evaluation (Irving, 1989).

In designing the evaluation, staff of the organisation will want to use some combination of these to collect the information they need. But first, of course, they need to know what it is they want to evaluate! Many centres begin their evaluation design by posing questions for each stage of the process. For example, at the pre-entry stage they may want to ask:

- What is the demand for the service?
- What are the most effective methods of promoting the service?
- What are the motivating forces of clients seeking the service?
- What orientation materials/sessions do individuals find useful?

Profiling

Are the self-assessment materials user-friendly?
How much time do advisors or mentors spend with the candidates/employees?
How long does it take individuals to complete the process?

Gathering evidence

What options are available to help candidates generate diverse evidence?
Are the portfolio development workshops cost-effective?
Do candidates from a particular field require special support?

Assessment and accreditation

How long does it take an assessor to review diverse evidence and complete the assessment?
What types of evidence do candidates present?
How many units were requested, assessed and accredited?

Post-assessment guidance

What type of new learning do candidates request?
Have candidates been satisfied with the service they have received?

Once the questions have been posed, staff will need to determine the best sources for collecting the information they need. Some possibilities include:

People	*Methods*
Candidates	Application forms
Advisors	Questionnaires
Mentors	Letters
Assessors	Discussions
Employers	Interviews
Centre managers	
Verifiers	
Support staff	

A number of points can serve to ease the actual data collection (Irving, 1989):

1. *Utilise existing systems whenever possible.*
Information that occurs normally as part of the on-going service can often yield information for both monitoring and evaluation. For example, application forms, minutes of meetings, workshop evaluation forms can all provide valuable quantitative and qualitative information.

2. *Consider the ease of collection.*
It is important not to impose extra work on staff or candidates. To do so may prevent them from completing other work, and there is also a high risk that they will not provide the information requested.

3. *Minute all team meetings.*
This can provide not only a rich source of information but also offer a historical perspective as the service develops. Often staff are surprised at how much they have accomplished in a relatively short time.

4. *Collect reasonable samples before the analysis begins.*
Organisations need to make sure enough candidates have completed the process before they begin the evaluation. Collecting information too soon or using a sample that is too small will not provide a realistic or accurate evaluation.

5. *Establish clear questions to be answered.*
The key to sound evaluation, just as in assessing candidates, is to ask the right questions. Only then can the organisation determine the best methods of collecting the sought-after information.

Linking implementation to monitoring and evaluation

In more successful organisations, monitoring and evaluation are intrinsic aspects of the implementation process itself. As we have seen earlier, this principle is found in Total Quality Management (TQM) systems. When information is collected, analysed and interpreted on an on-going basis, the centre is

- never 'shocked' by the outcomes of an evaluation;
- better prepared to deal with problems or issues while they are still manageable; and
- more able to make logical and cost-effective modifications to the service.

149

Summary

Implementing flexible assessment requires careful consideration of the organisational purpose and the strengths and structure of the organisation. Because the process is based on a number of assumptions not always found in traditional educational and training organisations or in employment contexts, an institutional audit needs to investigate the readiness and willingness of the staff to deliver the services. Ideally the audit should look at the centre's mission and objectives, its premises, its written and visual information, the skills and training needs of the staff, the availability of flexible learning options, the nature of the learners making use of the service, the framework by which learners progress through the system, costs and fees, and the management structure.

The outcomes of the audit may reveal points of tension between the needs of individuals and the administrative or resourcing needs of the organisation. The outcomes will also permit the centre to map out an action plan for overcoming obstacles, drawing on the strengths of the staff and designing an appropriate training programme by which staff will be able to offer the desired assessment services.

Monitoring and evaluating should be linked to the actual implementation of the service. By monitoring and evaluating the service on an on-going basis, the organisation will be well placed to address critical issues and improve the overall service and the effectiveness of the staff.

Chapter 7

Implications for Staff Development

Implementing flexible assessment strategies that embrace the concepts of APL offers significant challenges for those responsible for staff development. As we have seen throughout this book, there are a number of issues that need to be addressed before staff are competent to deliver the range of learning and assessment services required. They may need to develop in technical areas such as assessment and non-directive advising; equally they may need to improve in non-technical areas such as communication and their ability to work with others. In this chapter we will describe principles of best practice in flexible assessment staff development, provide guidance on basic topics and suggest outcomes for a range of training sessions. In the UK, of course, staff development in many contexts should reflect the TDLB standards, particularly since S/NVQ assessors must be accredited.

Principles of good practice

The first principle of good practice in flexible assessment training was described in the last chapter: the need for the organisational audit. Clearly a sound development strategy for staff cannot be developed without knowing the skills, knowledge and abilities of the staff within the organisation. Similarly, a training and development programme cannot be developed outside the parameters of the organisation's business plan and current and likely policies. Lastly, they cannot proceed without the commitment from the management of the organisation or centre to provide adequate resources to do the job.

These three requirements are equal partners in forming the basis of a sound flexible assessment service as shown in Figure 7.1.

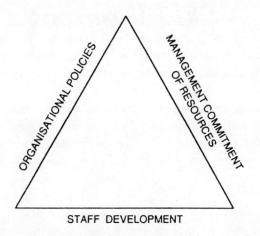

STAFF DEVELOPMENT

Figure 7.1 *The organisational requirements of a sound flexible assessment service*

If any one is lacking, there will be a high level of frustration among those who are trying to implement the service and an inherent weakness in the system.

Characteristics of an effective training programme

As far as possible, the training programme should be experientially based. Because there is so much 'doing' in the assessment process, many of the aspects are best understood by experiencing them first hand. The programme also needs to be highly interactive so staff members learn to work together and, as in all training, the purpose, objectives and expected learning outcomes must be clearly articulated and agreed among all the training participants.

Drawing on the principles of andragogy, both the trainee and the facilitator should assume responsibility for the content, timing, process and people to whom the training is offered. Andragogy is characterised by a belief that:

- the participants should accept the content of the programme based on evidence of need, not blind faith;
- participants should be active rather than passive;
- all participants have experience in the subject and therefore bring something with them to the training event;
- the participants have individual needs that must be addressed;
- discussion and experimentation are sound ways of fostering learning; and
- the participant should evaluate him- or herself.

During the training events, it is essential for the facilitators to build on the notions of andragogy. They need to engage the participants in aspects of the planning and/or the delivery of the training programme; they need to draw on the expertise of the group to develop the examples, activities and discussion points used in the training event. There should be ample time for individual reflection and small group discussions and various opportunities should be made available for the participants to evaluate their own progress and the overall training programme.

The primary job of the facilitator is to foster the development of each individual learner *and* the group. The sound delivery of assessment services is dependent on the strengths of each member of the assessment team and their ability to work effectively as a group. To no small degree this type of work generates a strong synergistic effect – that is, working together the group is capable of a far greater result than might be expected of single individuals. In planning any development activity this is a critical point for training staff to remember.

Having said that the facilitators are there to facilitate the development of the group and its individual members does not mean that the trainers can undertake the training without having a sound knowledge and some experience in the areas of assessment, advising and effective management. Although the group will do much problem-solving on its own, the facilitator must provide accurate and clearly defined input to serve as an appropriate stimulus for the group. The facilitator should also have an adequate knowledge of the concepts with relevant examples to draw on in order to respond to the workshop participants' questions and concerns.

A range of techniques
Experienced and effective facilitators try to use a range of techniques in their training programmes to promote experiential learning. As well as providing an interesting diversity for the participants, good facilitators recognise that people learn in different ways. Some people may find role plays, for example, an exciting way of trying out new concepts and behaviours. Others may be more comfortable working with written case studies followed by small group discussions. So, including a range of techniques in the training programme is not just of cosmetic value: diversity can provide an essential ingredient in helping individual participants to learn in the most effective ways they can.

There are many different techniques that can be used during an assessment training event. These include:

- case studies;
- demonstrations;
- role plays;
- simulations;
- games;
- observation;
- small group discussions;
- small group inquiry; and
- activity-based projects.

154

With all of these, however, the facilitator must prepare well in advance and be clear about the *reasons* for introducing each activity. It is also important to add that, for most sessions, the facilitator will need to provide some input to introduce the subject and provide a focus for the group work. As far as possible, the facilitator should try to involve participants even during these input sessions. A number of effective strategies can be used. For example, as part of the input session, the facilitator can ask the participants to define concepts, give their opinions about or describe some aspect of the content that would be of common interest to the group.

Good facilitation is central to an effective training event. Improperly facilitated activities can undermine the most cleverly designed training programme. A facilitator who is both knowledgeable and competent is an essential ingredient to ensuring an effective assessment training programme.

The more interesting and relevant the participants find the training event, the more likely it is that they will retain what they learn and grow in self-confidence to deliver one or more aspects of the service.

Clear learning outcomes
As with any good training programme, the trainers – and ideally, a small group of the people to be trained – need to set clear objectives for each portion of the training as well as for the overall training programme. These objectives, or expected learning outcomes as they are sometimes called, need to reflect behavioural outcomes whenever possible. A behavioural outcome suggests what the trainee will be able to *do* as opposed to simply *know* at the conclusion of the session. Drawing on the TDLB standards could prove useful in helping to set the objectives of the training programme. By way of example, the outcome statements might read something like that shown below.

At the end of this session participants will be able to *begin to*:

- agree and review a plan for assessing performance;

155

- collect and judge performance evidence against criteria;
- collect and judge knowledge evidence;
- make assessment decisions and provide feedback etc.

These statements, together with the respective performance criteria, clearly describe expected behaviour outcomes and serve as critical points of evaluation for both the participants and the trainer. (It should be noted of course that assessors and advisors will not be fully competent at the end of a given training session; full competence can only be achieved by performing in the workplace.)

Each individual at the end of the training will be able to assess whether or not he or she has achieved what they had hoped or planned to accomplish. In addition, the trainer can assess the effectiveness of the training strategies used to facilitate each person's progression. If most people feel they have achieved the outcome, then most likely the training programme will be considered successful.

It is worth noting that many training programmes do not specify expected learning outcomes in this way. Rather they either provide information about the *content input* or they offer non-behavioural objectives which may be difficult for both learner and trainer to assess. Consider the following examples:

In the training programme, the following topics will be covered:

- providing advice;
- providing assessment; and
- providing support materials for candidates.

Although this sort of approach gives participants a rough idea of the areas to be addressed, without expected learning outcomes participants have no way of knowing whether the training programme will be relevant to their needs. For example, the topic of 'providing advice' could be handled in any number of ways: at one end, it could simply provide information about the process; at the other extreme, it could offer an intensive experientially based learning opportunity for advisors already very experienced in candidate support and guidance. Also, input statements alone provide no framework by which either the learner or the trainer can evaluate whether or not the desired outcomes (whatever they were!) were met.

Similar problems arise when non-behavioural objectives are set. Consider this example:

At the conclusion of this training programme, the participants will . . .

- appreciate the characteristics of a portfolio development workshop;
- understand the principles of assessment; and
- know about assessment support materials.

Again, in and of themselves, there may be nothing wrong with statements such as these. However, how can 'appreciate', 'understand' or 'know' be assessed outside the context of doing?

Would it be sensible for the facilitator to develop paper and pencil tests when the whole point of flexible assessment training events is to help people become competent to deliver the various functions of the service? Equally important, how will the participants themselves know that they 'appreciate', 'understand' and 'know' unless they can apply what they know to the needs of a range of candidates and within an organisational context?

Well-written expected learning outcomes serve to inform the participants about the content and the level of the training session and also provide adequate standards by which they can measure their own development. It must be added, by the way, that if participants can successfully conduct a portfolio development workshop, they can also be judged to 'appreciate' the characteristics of a portfolio development workshop. Similarly if they can appropriately apply principles of assessment to a range of candidate evidence, it can also be judged that they 'understand' these principles, and so forth. No additional knowledge or understanding assessments may be needed.

Costs, time and facilities

Clearly costs, time and the nature of the training facilities are also important to the design of an effective flexible assessment training programme. As most professional trainers know, almost anything is possible – given enough time, money and staff!

However, in the case of flexible assessment, the training should be geared to meet the needs, both initial and on-going, of the people who are going to be involved in contributing to the delivery of the service. Ideally, these needs will have been identified during the organisational audit and the management will have committed sufficient resources – money, people and facilities – to allow the training staff to develop the training programme needed. However, most organisations operate in less than an ideal way, so the training staff must often make difficult decisions regarding the best use of the money, time and facilities available.

Training staff often have important partners in this decision-making process who are frequently overlooked: the participants themselves. If the participants can be part of the overall planning strategy for the training event, they can contribute not only ideas and suggestions prior to the event but will come to the event with a clear understanding of imposed constraints and limitations.

Developing the basic flexible assessment training sessions

There are several sessions around which almost all flexible assessment training events are organised. There are others which may be included, depending on the context in which the service is being offered and the prior experience of the workshop participants. In this section, key sessions are outlined and some possible learning outcomes suggested. Clearly, the staff responsible for the training will want to modify or adapt these to suit the needs of the likely participants.

At the outset it is assumed that the training event is being designed to enable people to *deliver* a range of advisory and assessment services. Although this event may be preceded by a briefing session to give people an overview of the assessment process, the sessions that follow are designed to prepare people to actually deliver the full range of services needed.

Normally, an assessment training event works best if there are no more than 25 participants. This is large enough to encourage diversity and interaction and small enough to ensure that each person can get what he or she needs from the event. Generally speaking, the training should include a good mix of those people who are to provide advice, assessment and management functions. Some organisations also find it is useful to include marketing, public relations and administrative staff, especially those who have responsibility for recording the outcomes of the assessment process. Each organisation, or consortium, will need to identify their own flexible assessment teams.

Experience suggests that it is best if the *entire* team undergoes the same training event, and that everyone covers all modules. Even though people serve different functions within the assessment process, it is critical to their effective work as a team and to the success of the programme for each not only to understand the other person's functions but to develop a sense of what it is like to *actually* provide that function. The more knowledgeable and skilled each member of the team is, the more likely it is that together they will be able to provide a coherent and learner-centred service. As with the basic notions of TQM and the Learning Organisation, each team member needs to become more aware of the roles and responsibilities of his or her fellow team members, respond more quickly and sensitively to their requests, and take their own learning and development more seriously.

One further word about who should be included in the training event. If support staff are not included in the primary sessions, it will be necessary to organise a second training event to meet their needs. Support staff, whether receptionists, secretaries, administrators, telephone operators, security guards or others, play a critical role in the delivery of assessment services. Since candidates regularly telephone, come in for appointments, request information, complete forms, etc, support staff need to be knowledgeable about the process, the needs of candidates, the advisors and the assessors, the resources required, fees charged and so forth. And beyond that, they need to understand as well as the staff who are actually delivering the services, why assessment services are important to the organisation, how they fit in with other offerings, and how they relate to the mission.

The basic training sessions

Within any given context, the exact number and length of sessions will vary considerably. However, suggested *minimum* times are provided to give the reader a rough idea of what may be required. These times assume that the workshop participants have some theoretical ideas about competence-based assessment and the candidates they are likely to work with, but no actual experience. Clearly, each of these sessions could be expanded (or contracted), depending on the needs of the group, the training time and resources available and the experience and professional judgement of the trainer. In addition, the actual training event could happen over varying lengths of time.

Introduction: 30 minutes

This session will allow the workshop participants and the trainer to introduce themselves. It should also allow the trainer to welcome the participants, to outline the training format and schedule and begin to create a friendly and effective learning environment. By the end of this session the participants should be able to:

- identify the trainer and other participants by name; and

- identify the purpose and framework of the event.

Adult learners: who they are and what they want: 1 hour
The purpose of this session is to introduce the basic principles of flexible assessment and begin to show its relevance and benefits to all learners, even those in the room! Since many people coming to training events often think that the service is only for those *not* in the room, it is often useful for the trainer to create or describe a theoretical situation that would require the participants to use a flexible assessment service and then ask them to identify aspects of their own past or current learning. It is also useful in this session to ask participants how they would prove to others that they really know and can do what they claim. By the end of the session, participants should be able to:

- describe the basic principles of APL in the context of a flexible assessment service;
- give examples of how they are themselves adult learners and possible candidates; and
- begin to raise issues about diverse evidence and assessment.

Beginning the process: 4 hours
This session should introduce participants to the basic principles and key features of APL (eg assessment not linked to any particular training or learning programme), and help them to see how these are integral to all flexible or competence-based assessment systems. Ideally it should allow them to work with the six-stage model, the continuum of assessment concept and the notion of diverse evidence. It should enable them to distinguish between the role of the advisor and that of the assessor. At the end of this session, participants should be able to:

- apply the basic principles of APL to flexible assessment strategies and systems;
- identify the meaning and application of diverse evidence;

- analyse the functions and responsibilities of advisors and assessors.

Providing advice to individuals: 3 to 5 hours

The purpose of this session is to give candidates an opportunity to explore one of the major roles of the advisor or mentor, that of providing advice and support to candidates. The session should allow the participants to develop the staged interview and use it with one another. By the end of this session, the participants should be able to:

- listen more effectively;
- use a range of techniques to encourage the candidate's reflection on past experiences and achievements;
- use a range of support materials, eg, checklists or learning outcome statements; and
- conduct a comprehensive interview, using a staged approach.

Developing the portfolio: 2 hours

This session should be designed to introduce participants to the concept of the portfolio and to give them an opportunity to identify examples of possible evidence. If possible, examples of strong and weak portfolios should be available for analysis and discussion. By the end of this session, the participants should be able to:

- describe the characteristics of a strong portfolio;
- identify possible sources of evidence; and
- begin to match diverse evidence to standards or learning outcomes.

Principles of assessment: 4 hours

Although the participants will already have begun to raise a number of issues related to assessment and diverse evidence, this session should focus on specific technical issues, eg, validity, sufficiency, currency, etc. It should also allow participants to distinguish between different forms of performance- and knowledge-based evidence, and encourage them to apply a range of assessment techniques to either role play or case study situations. By the end of the session, the participants should be able to:

- define and apply principles of assessment to diverse evidence;
- distinguish between performance- and knowledge-based evidence; and
- apply a range of techniques to role play or case study situations.

Reviewing the portfolio: 2 hours
This session should give participants hands-on experience of reviewing and recording the outcomes of portfolio segments. It should also allow them to identify direct and indirect evidence, address issues of consistency (reliability) and raise issues that they will want to deal with after they have processed a few portfolios of actual candidates. By the end of this session participants should be able to:

- systematically review a portfolio;
- record the outcomes of that review;
- develop a hypothetical initial assessment plan; and
- raise pertinent issues.

Giving feedback to candidates: 1½ hours
This session should be constructed to maximise the participants' opportunities to improve their overall communications skills, particularly their ability to listen and give constructive feedback. Both advisors and assessors need to be good communicators. This session should allow the participants to identify their strengths and development needs. At the end of this session participants should be able to:

- listen more effectively;

163

- respond to a range of diverse candidate needs;
- identify ways of giving feedback constructively and sensitively; and
- identify their own development needs in this area.

Developing the portfolio development workshop: 3 hours
In many respects this session can serve to synthesise key points from most of the previous sessions, because in developing the portfolio development workshop, participants must be able to facilitate the progression of the candidates in much the same way as they have been doing throughout the training event. This session should allow participants to develop a programme for delivering the portfolio development workshop and have an opportunity to identify various ways certain segments might be delivered. At the end of the session the participants should be able to:

- refine a draft programme for delivering a portfolio development workshop; and
- deliver the workshop to a range of candidates.

Developing support materials for candidates and the team:
2 hours
This session should allow participants to identify the support materials they will need for candidates and themselves. These may include such items as an application form, marketing leaflets, orientation materials, a guide to portfolio production, checklists based on the standards, recording forms for assessors, feedback forms for candidates to complete at the end of the process and so forth. At the end of this session participants should be able to:

- identify the support materials needed by candidates, advisors and assessors; and
- produce draft outlines for some of the materials.

Managing flexible assessment: 3–5 hours

This session should reflect the dominant working context of the participants. Workplace and education and training providers may have quite different needs. For example, workplace assessors may need to address issues like integrating assessment procedures into normal workplace practices, using the standards in the workplace, negotiating time to work on evidence collection or portfolio development for candidates with line managers, using external consultants and support, etc.

Education and training providers may need to focus on integrating flexible assessment strategies into normal provision, modifying policies and administrative procedures, marketing and promoting the service, shifting the roles and responsibilities of staff, etc.

The actual learning outcomes for each group may vary considerably even though the ultimate goal of each – to integrate and manage flexible assessment strategies – may be the same.

Team building and personal action planning: 3–5 hours

This session should encourage all those who are involved in the mentoring, supporting, assessment, administration and management of the service to consider how they can improve their internal communication, support their learners better and enhance their quality assurance processes. This is a critical session which should serve as a powerful reminder that team building and personal commitment are part of sustaining continuous improvement in the service. At the end of this session participants should be able to:

- identify key action points and time frames for implementing or improving the service;
- identify their own roles and responsibilities; and
- plan for further review and development.

Training sessions adapted from this basic framework will enable an organisation to implement an effective flexible assessment service. The exact content and times may vary, but assuming that

165

the training event is experientially based and the participants are committed to implementing the service, the organisation should have little difficulty in taking the work forward.

Expected outcomes of the training

By the end of the formal training period, the participants should be able to move back into their organisations to implement the service. As has been suggested, however, the team will need to meet regularly, match their progress to their agreed plans, and continue to revise and modify their implementation plans. In many respects, the most compelling and effective training occurs when the team begins working with actual candidates. It is only then that plans, progression routes and the quality of the advice, support and feedback can be realistically evaluated.

Optional sessions

To some readers the suggested training programme may seem like a heavy burden. Yet in many contexts this represents the minimum number of sessions needed and a variety of other optional sessions may also be required. The list below provides examples of these:

- Technical areas
    Setting standards or learning outcomes
    Ensuring quality through consistency and verification

- Flexible assessment process
    Supporting candidates
    Monitoring and evaluating the service
    Developing a range of briefing sessions
    Marketing the service to particular candidate groups

- Organisational
    Team building
    Investors in People
    Organisational change
    Integrating the standards in the workplace

Forming new partnerships
Total Quality Management
Modularising the curriculum

- Personal
Listening skills
Presentation skills
Leadership
Effective management
Mentoring

In addition to the main training event and any optional sessions, there are a number of other ways in which to continue staff development. Every team meeting is an opportunity for team members to learn from one another and explore issues; every new candidate provides an opportunity for the staff to face new issues and resolve problems; and every exchange between team members or those outside the team provides an opportunity to share perspectives and information.

Flexible assessment training is an ongoing activity. Because it is a service dedicated to the development of individuals, there is always something new to learn!

Summary

Staff development is essential to the successful implementation of flexible assessment services. To be effective, the training should reflect the needs of the staff to be trained and must include organisational policies and an adequate commitment of resources by senior managers. The training programme should be based on principles of andragogy, rather than pedagogy, and as such needs to be experientially based.

A range of training techniques can be used during the training event, for example case studies, role plays, simulations etc. Trainers or facilitators, however, must clearly identify the reason(s) for using one or more of these techniques and link

167

them to the expected learning outcomes. The learning outcomes themselves should describe behaviour outcomes which can be used as critical points of evaluation for both the participants and the trainers.

The basic training sessions should include a range of sessions geared to the needs of the participants. Whenever possible all members of the team need to participate in the training event; if support staff are not included in the primary sessions, additional training sessions need to be developed.

Chapter 8

Lessons Learned

Although this entire book has drawn on the experiences of many hundreds of people implementing flexible assessment systems in different countries, this last chapter offers a distillation of key lessons learned in recent years. It is hoped that these will serve as a summary checklist for those who are just starting out or those who are seeking continuous improvement in their work.

Planning the service*

● Be realistic! Set clear objectives and develop a work plan that is achievable. Make sure the plan is consistent with the mission or business strategy of the organisation. Build on existing systems and practices that are truly learner centred.

● Better to do a little well than a lot less well. Plan to pilot your flexible assessment services so you can evaluate new systems and procedures, motivate individuals to contribute their best, develop staff and explore resource implications in a controlled and systematic manner.

● Make sure clear assessable standards are in place. Whether they are called occupational standards, as in S/NVQs, or

---

* Many of the ideas presented in this chapter have been drawn from Cook (1991), Plummer (1991) and Simosko (1991).

learning outcomes, as in many higher education contexts, all flexible assessment centres need to have standards available for both candidates and the staff to use. Centres wanting to implement assessment services will need to develop standards if they are not already available.

• Draw on existing good practice. Seek out new ways of solving problems and meeting candidates' needs. Explore local networks, including in the UK such organisations as ITOs, TECs and Business Links. Explore international practices through the Internet, conferences, books and articles. The worldwide interest in flexible assessment issues continues to burgeon! Examples of good practice abound.

• Involve senior management in the planning. As was pointed out in Chapter 7, adequate resources are critical to the successful implementation of flexible assessment services. It is therefore essential that senior managers are *actively* involved in the planning of the service and are committed to fostering its development.

• Target client groups. In planning the service, it is important to know who the likely candidates will be. This is not just a marketing issue; it relates very much to the organisation's mission statement. This is particularly true in employer contexts: the introduction of flexible assessment services can be divisive if just a chosen few are offered new opportunities for learning and development.

Staff development

• Identify committed people who have a strong sense of responsibility. Develop champions. Cultivate creative team problem-solving and collaboration.

• Provide briefing and staff development opportunities for all staff, from senior managers to receptionists in colleges, and from mentors to line managers in the workplace. To ensure success, plan staff development activities, heighten awareness and provide opportunities to practise.

• Set and agree clear and realistic development objectives for all staff members who are to be involved in the service. Draw on concepts from Total Quality Management or the Learning Organisation to make sure that the objectives include those that spell out how different team members will support one another as well as the candidates. For example, assessors will need to provide support on a regular basis to the advisors or mentors.

• Clarify roles. Make sure that candidates, advisors/mentors, assessors and internal verifiers know their functions and stick to them! (If candidates are not aware of their responsibilities, it is hard work for everyone!)

• Evaluate the staff development needs of each member of the team. As a result of an organisational audit or through some other mechanism, make sure that the staff development activities take account of team members' previous experience – or the lack of it. For example, many assessors will not have had experience in using standards or drawing on diverse evidence as part of their assessments. And of course, in the UK, assessors need to work towards accreditation. Alternatively, advisors or mentors who are familiar with working with individuals in one particular context may find they need little development to extend their role in supporting candidates through the flexible assessment process.

• Set up networks to support staff and keep them in touch during the start-up phases of the work. This is especially important to establish a coherence in the team and ensure its ability to work effectively.

• Implement staff development opportunities once the service is up and running. These opportunities should include refresher training for staff who may not have been as involved as they would have liked; training for experienced people to tackle particular issues in more depth; and, of course, training for any new people who are to be involved in the future.

● Develop a strong team. Hold regular meetings with all staff to air problems, address issues and share successes.

Advising and supporting candidates

● Be patient with candidates. Not all candidates will be fully able to grasp the idea of accrediting prior learning or the notion of 'diverse evidence' at first. They may feel that there is something worth exploring but be unsure as to whether or not, or how, to proceed. Many candidates will need more time than might be anticipated to reflect on their skills and knowledge and determine the nature and sources of appropriate evidence. Providers should also remember that developing a portfolio is often a time-consuming process, and that presenting evidence for assessment purposes promotes learning. Learning and assessment take honest reflection and time.

● Create realistic expectations. Candidates will need to have a clear idea of their own responsibility in the process and be encouraged to take ongoing control of their own development and assessment. Advisors and mentors should certainly be prepared to support candidates but they should not be expected to fulfil unreasonable requests or be available at all hours of day or night.

● Be familiar with the standards or learning outcomes. It is just as important for advisors and mentors to be familiar with the standards or learning outcomes as the assessors. Although advisors will not be expected to have the technical knowledge of each area, they should have a general idea of both the level and the types of experiences candidates might have that would be relevant to particular sets of standards or learning outcomes. (They will need support and guidance from the assessors to do this well.)

• Give candidates honest feedback. If a candidate has no relevant experience or background in a particular area, the advisor or mentor needs to point that out when it is not self-evident to the candidate. Similarly, some candidates vastly undervalue their relevant experiences and accomplishments. The advisor should help each candidate develop a clear and accurate profile, giving appropriate feedback as consistently and sensitively as possible.

• Draw on a range of candidate experiences. There is a great tendency in some disciplines to encourage candidates to bring forward evidence from the workplace only. It is also important for advisors to try to stimulate candidates' thinking to include all their unpaid activities, from the home to volunteer work to uncertificated courses.

• Encourage peer-support groups. Especially when candidates are developing their portfolios or otherwise preparing for assessment, peer-support groups can provide an important extension to portfolio development or preparation-for-assessment workshops. Adults often prefer working together and can be of great assistance to one another. Peer support often helps to reduce the number of questions candidates bring to their advisors.

• Make sure guidelines for the construction of the portfolio are clear. Candidates often have so much material to put in their portfolios that organising it can be difficult. Advisors need to make sure that the written and oral guidelines are clear and consistent. Advisors should also plan to check each portfolio for completeness before sending it on for assessment.

• Communicate regularly with other advisors and assessors. Only through regular and open communication with other members of the team can advisors or mentors improve their skills and provide better support to candidates.

• Help candidates develop their own learning or training plans throughout the process. Advisors, like assessors, need to remember that flexible assessment is essentially about *developing* individuals, helping them reach their own targets. Although the assessment process may be an essential component of a candidate's overall development plan, there may be others that the organisation can facilitate as well.

Assessment

• Develop standards and learning outcomes. The subject specialists within an organisation need to assume responsibility for this although, as was pointed out in Chapter 7, the staff development unit may need to organise the training to facilitate the standards development work.

• Develop checklists as appropriate. For some groups of candidates it may be easier to use checklists to review their strengths rather than the standards or learning outcomes themselves (which are not always presented in the most user-friendly fashion). In these cases, the assessors will need to use the standards or learning outcomes to prepare checklists which relate more directly to candidates' actual experience.

• Provide guidance about evidence. Initially many candidates may be tempted to provide an excess of evidence. Every effort should be made by the centre, and in particular the assessors, to provide guidelines which will help candidates develop the *minimum* amount of evidence needed. Quality, not quantity, should be the message.

• Avoid over-assessing. Many assessors lacking confidence ask candidates to generate evidence using many different techniques, eg portfolio evidence, demonstration and oral questioning. Although it may be necessary to assess some aspects of a candidate's competence or strengths in one or more ways, assessors need to focus again on the *minimum* amount of information they need to be sure the candidate has reached the standard. Over-assessing creates unnecessary work for both the assessor and the candidate and it costs money!

● Consider all types of evidence. Many new assessors are surprised by the range of quality evidence candidates bring forward. Assessors need to keep an open mind about the diverse evidence candidates *could* bring forward, as long as it meets the standards or learning outcomes.

● Meet with other assessors and the advisors on a regular basis. As for the advisors, the best way for assessors to develop and address key issues is to work with their colleagues!

Marketing the service

● Avoid jargon. Find ways of describing the service which will motivate potential candidates. This suggestion applies to other information and services that may be connected with the assessment service too. Since many candidates will have been away from formal education or training for a long time, they may be unfamiliar with many of the concepts and words professional educators and trainers take for granted. Clear, easy to read language will help them understand what is on offer.

● Raise awareness. Target specific client or employee groups and emphasise the relevance and the benefits of the assessment process. This may require developing more than one set of leaflets, for example, to describe the service. As appropriate, special attention should be given to the needs of disadvantaged groups and/or those with special needs.

● Put the service in context. Although flexible assessment may need to be marketed as a separate service in the beginning, whenever possible it should be linked to other programmes and services. The *idea* of valuing and recognising peoples' strengths and fostering personal development should be recognised in the organisation's mission statement and its public commitment to fostering lifelong learning and continuous improvement.

● Publicise the successes of flexible assessment. Success breeds success. Capitalise on the positive outcomes of the flexible assessment service and use those to spread the word.

● Use a variety of marketing and promotion approaches. Experience has shown that one is seldom enough. It is best to draw attention to the benefits of the service in as many ways as is possible.

Costs and fees

● Build cost-effective practices into the flexible assessment service. For example, working with groups of candidates, developing user-friendly self-assessment materials, forming partnerships with others outside the organisation, may all serve to reduce costs. In employment contexts, staff may need to be given time to generate evidence and/or work on their portfolios.

● Expect the time staff spend with candidates to be reduced with experience. Advisors and assessors are often surprised at how much less time their jobs take per candidate once they have experience. Not only do experienced advisors and assessors know more about the flexible assessment process and the candidates they work with, they also have greater self-confidence in their decisions. This in turn seems to reduce the time they need to spend on each phase of the process.

● Try not to cut corners to reduce costs. In the long run it will be better, and more cost effective, if the organisation develops a comprehensive, learner-centred service. For example, it is essential that staff are available to candidates at convenient times, eg, after 5 pm, whether in person or through technology. Disappointed or demotivated candidates won't continue.

● Introduce a fee structure that is clear and easy to understand. Regardless of the type of fee structure an education or training provider introduces, candidates should be able to understand what they are paying for. Charging candidates for separate services, eg, advice, portfolio development workshop(s) and assessment may be one way to ensure this clarity. And please note: charges for assessment must be related to units *assessed*, not to units credited! (The same level of work is involved in assessing a particular unit, whether or not the candidate receives credit for it. Additionally a centre that charges for units credited could be accused of having an ulterior motive in making sure candidates succeed.)

Organisational change

● Integrate flexible assessment services into existing systems and procedures. Candidates need to understand how they can learn and develop – and how assessment is an integral part of that process.

● Consider the learners' needs. As part of the organisational audit or other mechanism, take a fresh look at the environment, the delivery structures and systems, staffing levels and time-tables, administrative services, opening hours and information services. The nature and quality of each of these could have a significant impact on the development and implementation of the flexible assessment service.

● Encourage ownership of the flexible assessment service. Encourage people throughout the organisation to learn about the service, ask questions and contribute ideas. Be sure to recognise the achievements of each individual contributing to the service – even just a 'thank you' can go a long way to keeping people committed to doing their best!

Forming links

● Build on existing links. In today's world, most organisations already work with a range of other organisations and partners. These might include companies, unions, associations, professional bodies, libraries, colleges and universities, government agencies, training providers, consultants, etc. Many of these existing links will be useful to organisations implementing flexible assessment and learning services. Not only can they serve as potential sources of candidates, they might also be willing to commit valuable resources to the development of the service.

● Establish new links. Sometimes providers find it necessary to develop new links to deliver assessment services effectively. For example, if the centre is a traditional educational provider, the staff might find it beneficial to work with one or more employers to identify large pools of candidates. Similarly, if the provider is an employer, its staff might find that a local college is able to provide open or distance learning options or short 'top-up' courses for its employees. Employers also often form networks.

Employers as providers

● Introduce flexible assessment services to motivate staff to meet future needs. Link the process to annual appraisals, training needs analysis, personal development programmes, and other business improvement initiatives.

● Identify likely benefits to the organisation. Based on the experience of other employers, there is a broad range of benefits to be considered. Flexible assessment services can:

- integrate personal development with organisational needs;
- foster better use of training resources;
- reward employees for their accomplishments;
- promote the upgrading of skills;
- create a more flexible and self-confident workforce; and
- improve performance.

Quality assurance

• Develop a quality assurance system. In many contexts, flexible assessment services will be a new idea. It will therefore be important for the providing centre to demonstrate on an on-going basis that it is not offering a 'cheap' or 'easy' route to credit or qualifications. Establishing a quality assurance system *within* the organisation may be just as important as establishing one that includes external verifiers.

• Identify the relevant external organisations early on in the planning. Depending on the level and context in which the service is to be offered, a number of different agencies may be involved in the quality assurance or verification process. If possible, they should participate in any planning or staff development events and should be notified as soon as the service is operational.

• Keep records carefully. An important aspect of any quality assurance system is having information available to those who will monitor and/or evaluate the service. Centres will want to develop and provide information about the training of their staff, the methods by which candidates were assessed and the outcomes of all assessments. For each of these, centres will need to develop recording forms and efficient storage and retrieval systems.

• Monitor the outcomes of assessments. As part of quality assurance, it will be important for the centre to monitor the outcomes of each assessment, to keep a record of the units assessed and accredited, and to retain complete information on the nature of each assessment for each candidate.

• Set up consistency checks. The work of each individual assessor should be monitored to make sure that standards are being interpreted similarly and that evidence is being used consistently. A centre may want to have more than one assessor review and assess a small sample of portfolios or other diverse evidence periodically to see if the independent judgements made by each assessor are comparable.

● Monitor the progression of candidates. Candidates' success offers the most valuable quality assurance data of all. It is therefore essential that centres monitor candidates' progression after they complete their work. A range of questions might be asked: How well do candidates do in more advanced training or learning situations? Are they able to qualify for promotions in their jobs? Are they able to enter the job market for the first time? Can they be admitted to programmes offering professional qualifications? Each organisation will need to identify the key questions to ask about its candidates and, as a matter of course, introduce these early on during implementation.

Summary

There is much to be learned from the experience of others who have successfully implemented flexible assessment services. Although not all the ideas presented in this chapter will be relevant to all readers, it is hoped that they will serve to highlight and synthesise many of the ideas presented in earlier chapters. It is hoped too that these 'lessons learned' will provide challenging examples of how flexible assessment can be integrated into organisations and the communities they serve to the benefit of staff and candidates alike.

Appendix

The S/NVQ Revolution

National Vocational Qualifications (NVQs) and Scottish Vocational Qualifications (SVQs) have brought sweeping changes to the vocational education and training infrastructure of Great Britain. They represent a conceptual shift in the way individuals' skills are recognised. As a result, they have been the catalyst for a host of developments in the delivery of vocational training and assessment. Most important, S/NVQs have closely linked education and training provision to the economic needs of the country.

Where did S/NVQs come from?

In 1981 the MSC paper *A New Training Initiative: An Agenda for Action* highlighted that 'Britain needs a flexible, adaptable workforce to cope with the uncertainties which cloud the future'.

In an era of growing international competition and rapidly changing technologies, Britain's vocational education and training provision was found to be deficient in comparison with those of many nations. The *Agenda for Action* outlined a strategy for improving the skills of young people and adults through training. Central to the *New Training Initiative* was the development of 'standards of a new kind'.

The 1986 White Paper *Working Together – Education and Training* (DE, 1986) detailed how these developments were to come about. Standards reflecting the performance expected in the work place would be defined. These new kinds of standards were termed standards of competence. The Manpower Services Commission (MSC) was charged with leading the development work and the National Council for Vocational Qualifications (NCVQ) was established to bring about the reform of vocational qualifications using standards to create a cohesive framework. In Scotland, the Scottish Vocational Education Council (SCOTVEC) took this role to introduce SVQs.

The notion of competence

The notion of competence had grown from those earlier imperatives of a flexible and adaptable workforce, and in essence described the ability to perform to the level expected in employment. Definitions of competence have evolved, but might be stated as:

> The ability to apply knowledge, understanding and skills in performing to the standards required in employment, including solving problems and meeting changing demands. (Beaumont, 1996)

Since standards of competence reflect what people are expected to do in the workplace, they are written to reflect the outcomes of performance. Achievement of an S/NVQ is not therefore tied to a period of learning or input as most vocational qualifications have been in the past. Standards of competence are criterion-referenced and explicit so that they lend themselves readily to assessment and a host of other uses.

Setting the standards

Perhaps for the first time, the providers of vocational education and training worked with the users – employers and other industry representatives – to define the standards. Industry Training Organisations and a wide range of other interested parties came together to establish Industry Lead Bodies (ILBs, later 'Lead Bodies') to lead work to develop and review standards in their sector. As the national effort got underway, the MSC drew up an occupational map to monitor the development of standards across all vocational sectors and to ensure a comprehensive coverage.

Standards were set through the process of *functional analysis*. This involved groups of employer representatives working together to identify the functions and activities performed in a particular occupational area. The standards were defined by systematically expressing 'what needs to happen next for this to be achieved'. Standards development groups were challenged to devise a rounded and encompassing description of competence which included knowledge and understanding, practical skills, contingency management, and personal skills across a representative range of contexts and circumstances. Importantly, the standards also were designed to reflect evolving and future employer expectations. Once developed, Lead Bodies are required periodically to review and revise their standards to ensure that S/NVQs continue to be relevant and to meet changing employer needs.

The Standards Programme represented a concerted national effort to set in place competences appropriate to all Britain's workforce and it continued well into the mid-1990s. By 1996, 87% of workers had access to S/NVQs.

National Targets for Education and Training (NTETs)

NTETs were first launched in 1991 at the instigation of the Confederation of British Industry (CBI). Separate but related Targets were set for Scotland. The aim was to improve the nation's competitiveness by raising standards and attainment levels in education and training to world class levels. Progress towards NTETs is reported annually, and based on achievements so far, NTETs were revised in 1995. A number of the Targets relate specifically to S/NVQ achievement. For example, Lifetime Learning Target 1:

60% of the workforce to be qualified to S/NVQ Level 3 (or equivalent) by the year 2000.

NTETs have proved a driving force behind the growing take up of S/NVQs, particularly through the work of Training and Enterprise Councils (TECs).

The role of NCVQ

Lead Bodies work with the NCVQ and awarding bodies to
structure standards of competence into S/NVQ form. To be
accredited as an S/NVQ an award must be:

- based on national standards required for performance in
  employment, and take into account future needs with regard
  to technology, markets and employment;
- based on assessment of the outcomes of learning, normally
  arrived at independently of any particular mode, duration or
  location of learning;
- awarded on the basis of valid and reliable assessment, which
  ensures that performance to the national standards can be
  achieved at work;
- free from overt and covert discriminatory practices.

S/NVQs are placed within a framework of 13 occupational areas
and five Levels of achievement. The S/NVQ Framework is
designed to simplify the provision of vocational qualifications
across a broad spectrum and to promote progression through the
Levels. Level 1 for example, represents largely routine activities,
while Level 5 involves complex competences across a broad range
of unpredictable contexts. Details of all S/NVQs within the
framework are contained on the National Database of Vocational
Qualifications produced by NCVQ. The Database may be pur-
chased and also is accessible at a very broad range of local points,
including colleges, libraries, and careers offices.

What do S/NVQs look like?

All S/NVQs take a common format. In addition to a title, each
comprises

- Units of Competence
- Elements of Competence
- Performance Criteria
- Range statements
- Knowledge specifications
- Evidence requirements

Units of Competence Every S/NVQ is made up of a number of units of competence. Each of these is a complete statement of competence that has independent value in employment. Units of Competence are available for independent accreditation. Many have a unit descriptor that defines their relationship with other Units in the S/NVQ. Units are made up of a number of elements of competence.

Elements of Competence describe something an individual working in a particular occupational area should be able to do. Each may be expressed as an activity or outcome that must be demonstrable so that it may be assessed. An element relates to others within a single unit.

Performance Criteria describe the quality of outcomes expected in the performance of an element of competence and also reflect critical features in the way the activity must be performed. Performance Criteria provide the measures against which competent performance of an element may be assessed.

Range Statements are attached to each element of competence and describe the circumstances and contexts across which an individual must be able to perform the standards if they are to be considered occupationally competent. Range statements frequently cover location, environment, equipment, and/or materials.

Knowledge Specifications are included in every element of competence and cover facts, theories, principles, and requirements related to the application of knowledge in performance. Only knowledge that supports performance can be specified. Through assessment, knowledge specifications enable candidates to show that they can transfer performance across a breadth of situations.

Evidence Requirements specify the evidence necessary for a satisfactory judgement to be made about an individual's competence. They specify: the minimum performance evidence required; other types of necessary evidence and/or timescales for assessment; acceptable assessment methods; and any restrictions relating to assessment, eg, on the use of simulation.

S/NVQs are composed primarily of mandatory units, though during the later stages of the Standards Programme increasing numbers of S/NVQs included optional units or offered additional units. These increase the flexibility of S/NVQs, take into account specialist functions, and support career development. A proportion of S/NVQs have common units which are also included in S/NVQs from other occupational areas, such as Management units of competence. These enable individuals to progress and to transfer to other contexts.

Assessing S/NVQs

Just as S/NVQs are based on a new kind of standard, so approaches to assessment are different in a number of respects. In contrast to traditional norm-referenced assessment, the new standards:

- are criterion referenced so that assessment decisions are based on evidence judged against specified criteria rather than through comparisons with others;
- are explicit, so that the candidate is fully aware of the criteria against which he or she will be assessed;
- are not linked to any particular learning programme, so evidence may be drawn from a wide variety of sources;
- reflect workplace requirements – this will be the primary source for evidence.

For all these reasons and others, an S/NVQ candidate has considerable knowledge of and control over the assessment process. In many respects, the candidate-led, flexible assessment systems used today have evolved from the concepts and application of APL (see Preface).

Performance evidence is required for every element of competence. This can be reflected in a product, or through observation or witness testimony. Simulations are also permissible in some circumstances. Evidence of knowledge and understanding across the contexts described in the range statements will also be required, and may be elicited through oral questioning, projects or assignments, as well as through performance evidence. Evidence may be applicable across a number of elements of competence and should not be re-assessed. S/NVQs allow for a diversity of evidence to be brought forward, and of course evidence of prior learning may form an important source of evidence for many individuals.

Assessment decisions are based on the combination of evidence brought forward. To be successful, candidates should provide sufficient evidence that:

- includes performance evidence for each element;
- demonstrates the candidate's knowledge, understanding and ability to apply it;
- consistently satisfies all performance criteria;
- covers all aspects of the range statement;
- fulfils the evidence requirements; and
- reflects current competence.

The cost-effectiveness and practicality of assessment is a key consideration. Commonly, portfolios are used to organise and present evidence. This approach ensures that assessment is candidate-led and can save time for both candidates and assessors through the use of diverse evidence and cross-referencing. This process readily integrates evidence of prior learning and is developed from early APL work in Britain. Portfolio development can be onerous for some candidates and may be less suitable in some occupational areas, however, and other approaches are equally permissible.

For organisations, the design of S/NVQ assessment is intended to allow for local flexibility and integration into existing systems, most particularly in the workplace. In keeping with the aims and principles of S/NVQs, assessment should be highly relevant to the objectives and needs of the organisation and individual candidates. Assessment should not be a burden.

Quality assurance

Quality assurance of S/NVQs and their delivery is the shared responsibility of the NCVQ, awarding bodies, Approved Centres and their representatives, and assessors.

NCVQ works with awarding bodies to establish and monitor S/NVQ accreditation and quality assurance systems. The NCVQ has published a 'Common Accord' guidance document to promote best practice and consistency in quality assurance across awarding bodies.

Awarding bodies accredit S/NVQs and monitor and quality assure the assessment and support systems of those organisations which they approve to deliver them. **External Verifiers** are employed representatives of awarding bodies who carry out monitoring visits and sample assessments. They themselves must be accredited with the S/NVQ unit relating to external verification.

Approved Centres are approved by an awarding body to offer S/NVQ assessment. They are required to comply with rigorous criteria to earn this approval and are monitored by their awarding body to ensure that they maintain these standards. **Internal Verifiers** quality assure internal assessments by sampling the work of assessors. They must themselves be accredited with the S/NVQ unit relating to internal verification.

Assessors carry out S/NVQ assessment. They must have a credible background in the vocational area in which they are assessing candidates, and also must be accredited with the appropriate S/NVQ units for assessors.

For a more detailed discussion of assessment and quality assurance principles, see Chapter 5.

S/NVQ delivery

S/NVQs were designed to be delivered in a wide variety of non-traditional contexts and often by organisations that previously did not offer accreditation. Further and Higher Education establishments and other traditional provider organisations continue to offer S/NVQs and learning programmes aligned to S/NVQ achievement. For many, the demands of the S/NVQ system, requiring ready access to flexible assessment, have proved highly challenging. Private training providers frequently have found the transition easier, perhaps through involvement in government training schemes that were geared towards S/NVQs. Such organisations were better able to adapt their provision because they tended to focus on a few S/NVQs in the occupational areas in which they specialised.

Increasingly, employer organisations have themselves become deliverers of S/NVQ assessment and related learning opportunities. TECs (Local Enterprise Councils (LECs) in Scotland) have played an important role in fostering and supporting employer involvement in S/NVQ provision. Many employers have developed partnerships with local colleges or other providers. Others (particularly small employers) have formed consortia and become Approved Centres. In a few occupational areas, eg care, it is mandatory for those implementing S/NVQs to belong to such a consortium. Many larger employer organisations have themselves become Approved Centres with in-house assessors and verifiers. Some even offer their assessment services to other employers.

S/NVQs in the workplace

Increasing numbers of employers are introducing S/NVQs, not just for accreditation purposes but for the benefit of the organisation as a whole. National standards of competence have proved a highly flexible and effective tool in improving business performance. Standards can be applied across a wide range of activities that include:

- reviewing and defining job roles and job descriptions;
- recruiting and selecting employees;
- target setting, for individuals and the organisation;
- identifying skills shortages;
- analysing training needs;
- evaluating and designing training programmes;
- appraising and assessing individuals;
- career planning; and
- reviewing and improving organisational systems and procedures.

Some employers have found that the national standards can be used so widely that they promote consistency and provide a common language across the organisation. The benefits have proven to include:

- improved business performance;
- increased productivity by individual employees;
- the introduction of new and improved ways of doing things;

189

- improved flexibility and transferability within the work force;
- more focused and effective in-house training;
- reduced costs and time associated with training and assessment activities;
- improved team working;
- increased employee motivation;
- higher employee confidence; and
- prestige and marketing opportunities of a 'qualified work force'.

For individual employees, benefits might include:

- improved performance;
- recognition of existing competence;
- higher self-esteem and self-awareness of skills;
- increased confidence to participate and 'add value' at work;
- enhanced progression and transfer opportunities;
- improved management and organisational skills; and
- greater motivation towards personal development.

Many employers also provide S/NVQ accreditation opportunities for their staff, so that they have the chance to gain a marketable qualification.

As with any new system, the introduction of national standards and S/NVQs has proved time-consuming and resource-intensive for some employers. The experience of those who have become involved so far has highlighted that:

- organisation-wide commitment (particularly the endorsement of senior managers) is essential;
- standards and S/NVQs are most effective when integrated with organisational systems and procedures;
- those using the standards need time and support to come to terms with their language and competence-based systems; and
- the benefits may take time to emerge.

Experience also suggests that in the long-term the benefits brought by national standards and NVQs can far outweigh the costs.

Other developments

GNVQs
These are broad based qualifications that follow the same format as S/NVQs but which describe national standards for vocational education. Usually offered by colleges and schools, GNVQs provide an alternative route to further vocational qualifications or employment, particularly for young people over the age of 16 years. GNVQs do not relate directly to S/NVQ units and are broader in scope; they therefore do not offer direct progression to the S/NVQ framework.

Key skills
Key skills underpin competent performance and frequently enable individuals to transfer across different situations. Many of the standards on which S/NVQs are based include key skills, though often these are not stated explicitly. The NCVQ has developed a number of key skills units which are available for separate accreditation, including Communication, Application of Number, Information Technology, and Personal Skills – Working with Others. Achievement in key skills features heavily in the NTETs for Foundation Learning. Based on research into key skills and employer needs, it is anticipated that as S/NVQs are up-dated they will include more explicit core skill requirements.

Investors in People
This is a national quality standard aimed at promoting and fostering effective investment in training and development by employers towards achieving business goals. Employer organisations are assessed against the Investors in People standards and must demonstrate their commitment to the development of all people and provide evidence of the systems and procedures in place to action this commitment. The Investors in People kite mark has achieved considerable status and in July 1995 more than one quarter of the UK's workforce was employed by organisations which had achieved or were working towards the Investors in People standard.

S/NVQs in the future

The review of 100 S/NVQs

A Government White Paper, *Competitiveness – Helping Business to Win* (May, 1994), brought about a review of the 100 most used S/NVQs. This involved employers, candidates, provider organisations, awarding bodies, and all other interested parties in intensive consultation. The review found widespread support for the concepts and benefits brought by S/NVQs among employers. It also highlighted several areas for improvement including in the quality and cost-effectiveness of assessment, the flexibility of S/NVQ format and structures, the language of S/NVQ standards, and in the amount of information employers received about S/NVQ developments. The government published an Action Plan in response to the so-called Beaumont Report (NCVQ/ScotVEC, 1996), which also served to focus the ongoing review of all S/NVQs (to be completed by 1998). In its plan the government confirmed its commitment to S/NVQs and outlined measures to reduce bureaucracy, increase rigour in assessment, and improve the fit of S/NVQ-related systems to employer needs and circumstances. The Action Plan introduced the notion of a 'User's Charter', a statement reflecting the services customers of S/NVQ deliverers can expect to receive and a mechanism by which they can seek redress if they are dissatisfied.

Progress towards NTETs

The NTETs' annual reports highlight that while significant progress towards NTETs is being achieved, some Targets are unlikely to be reached unless more can be done to gain the commitment and action of employers. Future plans include increased promotion of S/NVQs through industry bodies, with a greater focus on the needs of different sectors. Promotion of the business benefits of S/NVQs and related activities such as Investors in People are seen as an important way forward.

Summary

S/NVQs were conceived in the early–mid 1980s as a device for improving the skills and flexibility of the UK's workforce. They are based on standards of competence which reflect the ability to apply the skills, knowledge and understanding in performing to the standards expected in the workplace. S/NVQs reflect the outcomes of performance and are not tied to any course of learning. They are explicit and criterion-referenced and therefore lend themselves to assessment. The standards were set by employer representatives through a process known as functional analysis. Standards were structured into S/NVQ format by Industry Lead Bodies, together with awarding bodies and the NCVQ (or Scot-VEC), which had been established to lead the development of the new S/NVQ framework. By 1996, 87% of workers had access to S/NVQs. The National Targets for Education and Training were launched to increase levels of attainment in education and training, at least partly through S/NVQs.

All S/NVQs take the same format. They are based on units of competence, which in turn are comprised of elements of competence with associated performance criteria, range statements, evidence requirements, and knowledge specifications. S/NVQs may be assessed using diverse evidence, although performance evidence is required against each element of competence. Evidence of prior learning is frequently included as part of the combination on which assessment decisions are made. Assessment is a candidate-led process, often through the use of portfolios as a way of organising and presenting diverse evidence. Rigorous quality assurance procedures have been set in place and assessors and verifiers involved in the delivery of S/NVQs themselves are required to be qualified with the appropriate S/NVQ units.

S/NVQs were designed to be delivered in a variety of non-traditional contexts and while colleges and private training providers continue to offer them, employers are increasingly introducing S/NVQs themselves. Frequently this involves partnership arrangements, such as consortia or joint ventures with Approved Centres. Employers are also benefitting from the introduction of the national standards, which offer a useful tool in improving business performance and motivating and rewarding employees. However, NTETs' progress reports highlight that the take up of S/NVQs still falls short of what is necessary if we are to compete in the international marketplace. Increasing S/NVQ implementation by employers is recognised as the way forward. Ten years after the

introduction of S/NVQs, the review of those most used highlighted ways in which S/NVQs might be further aligned to the needs of
employers and the workforce.

References

Astin, A W, Anouje, C J and Korn, W S (1986) *Evaluation of the CAEL Student Potential Program*, Council for Adult and Experiential Learning, Chicago.

Beaumont, G (1996) *Review of 100 NVQs and SVQs*, NCVQ/SCOTVEC.

CAEL (1975) *CAEL Working Paper No. 6 – A Guide for Assessing Prior Experience through Portfolios*, Cooperative Assessment of Experiential Learning, Educational Testing Service, USA.

Care Sector Consortium (1990) *Draft Occupational Standards: Pilot Edition*, Care Sector Consortium.

CBI (1989) *Towards a Skills Revolution: Report of the Vocational Education and Training Taskforce*, Confederation of British Industry, London.

Cook, C (1991) APL – What Have we Learnt? Practical Lessons from Recent Development Projects in the UK, unpublished paper produced for the Employment Department, Sheffield.

Cross, K P (1981) *Adults as Learners: Increasing Participation and Facilitating Learning*, Jossey-Bass, San Francisco.

Covey, S R (1992) *The Seven Habits of Highly Effective People*, Simon & Schuster, London.

Cross, K P (1986) *Adults as Learners*, Jossey-Bass, San Francisco.

De Board, R (1989) *Counselling Skills*, Wildwood House Ltd, Hampshire.

DE (1986) *Working Together – Education and Training*, Department of Employment White Paper, Cmnd 9823, HMSO, London.

Dewey, J (1938) *Experience and Education*, Collier, New York.

Docking, R A (1990a) *Assessment in the Workplace: Facts and Fallacies*, Department of Productivity and Labour Relations, Western Australia.

Docking, R A (1990b) An A–Z of Assessment Myths and Assessment in the Workplace, paper presented at the TAFE National Center for Research and Development Conference, Assessment and Standards in Vocational Education and Training, Adelaide.

ED (1990) *Accreditation of Prior Learning: A Training Agency Perspective*, Employment Department, Sheffield.

ED (1991) *A Guide to the TECs Advertising Campaign*, Employment Department, Sheffield.

Gamson, Z F (1989) *Higher Education and the Real World*, Longwood, Wolfeboro, New Hampshire.

Gould, R (1978) *Transformations: Growth and Change in Adult Life*, Simon & Schuster, New York.

Hall, J (1991) *APL for Experienced Managers: Final Report*, MCI, London.

HMSO (1981) A *New Training Initiative: a Programme for Action*, HMSO, London.

Irving, G (1989) Developing a Systematic Approach to APL, unpublished thesis, Northern College of Education.

Kanter, R M (1985) *The Change Masters*, Unwin Paperbacks, London.

Kendall, P (1990) Costing and Pricing APL, unpublished training material, Filton Technical College.

Knowles, M S (1970) *The Modern Practice of Adult Education: Andragogy versus Pedagogy*, Association Press, New York.

Kolb, D A (1976) *Learning Styles Inventory: Technical Manual*, McBer and Company, Boston.

Levinson, D, Darrow, C N, Klein, E G, Levinson, M H and McKee, B (1978) *The Seasons of a Man's Life*, Knopf, New York.

Manpower Services Commission (MSC) (1981) A *New Training Initiative: Agenda for Action*, HMSO, London.

MCI (1991) *Management Standards: Implementation Pack*, Management Charter Initiative, London.

Michalak, D F and Yager, E G (1979) *Making the Training Process Work*, Harper and Row, New York.

Michelson, E and Mandell, A (1988) *Approaches to Portfolio Development Workshops*, CAEL, Chicago.

Mitchell, L and Johnson, C (1987) Selecting Suitable Methods of Assessment (working paper prepared for MSC/NCVQ Technical Advisory Group, Sheffield), in Simosko, S (1988) *Assessing Learning: A CAEL Handbook for Faculty*, CAEL, Chicago.

OU (1990) *APL: An Open Learning Pack for Advisors and Assessors*, Open University, Milton Keynes.

Parsloe, E (1992) *Coaching, Mentoring and Assessing: a Practical Guide to Developing Competence*, Kogan Page, London.

Plummer, R (1991) A *Guide for Advisors*, Management Charter Initiative, London.

Simosko, S (1988) *Assessing Learning: A CAEL Handbook for Faculty*, CAEL, Chicago.

Simosko, S (1990) *Final Report: Identifying, Assessing and Recording the Personal Competences of Young People*, Employment Department, Sheffield.

Simosko, S (1991) A *Guide for Assessors*, Management Charter Initiative, London.

Simosko, S (1992) *Embedding Accreditation of Prior Learning (APL)*, Competence & Assessment Briefing Series, Number 7, October 1992, Employment Department, Sheffield.

Simosko, S (1995) *PLA and Educational Reform: a Vision for Now*, The Centre for Curriculum and Professional Development, Victoria, BC.

Stewart, J (1990) Assessor's Notes, unpublished paper, Sheffield.

Tjok-a-Tam, S (1991) *The Forgotten Manager*, Management Charter Initiative, London.

Warren, J R and Breen, P W (1976) *The Educational Value of Portfolio and Learning Contract Development*, CAEL, Chicago.

Index